ALSO BY
LAWRENCE EARL

Yangtse Incident

(1951)

THIS IS A BORZOI BOOK,
PUBLISHED BY ALFRED A. KNOPF

THE

BATTLE

OF

BALTINGLASS

Lawrence Earl

THE

Battle

O F

Baltinglass

Alfred A. Knopf: New York: 1953

L. C. catalog card number: 52–12196

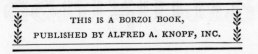

THIS IS A BORZOI BOOK,
PUBLISHED BY ALFRED A. KNOPF, INC.

FIRST AMERICAN EDITION

FOR

ANNA

✿

My chief in the late war, Field-Marshal Mont-
gomery, used to describe a battle as
    the assault,
        the dogfight,
            and the pursuit. . . .
MAJOR-GENERAL MEADE EDWARD DENNIS,
    in a speech to the Baltinglass Protest Committee

PREFACE

THE BATTLE OF BALTINGLASS was an adventure in democracy which actually did take place. Because it is not fiction I lacked the happy licence of the novelist who arranges his facts to suit his plot, who can plumb the minds of his characters, enter locked doors, and eavesdrop on deep secrets. Still, with the friendly co-operation of the people of Baltinglass, I was able to explore events as they occurred; and I should like to thank them all, on both sides of the battle. I also thank the editors of the *Irish Press*, the *Irish Times*, and *Parliamentary Debates, Dáil Éireann* (*Official Report*), for permission to quote from their columns; and the publishing department of Waltons' Musical Galleries, in Dublin, for permission to quote from the song *The Battle of Baltinglass*.

One small point, which readers may notice, needs explanation. Miss Helen Cooke, round whom the battle swirled, is variously reported herein to range from forty-six to fifty-five years of age.

"I was fifty-five years of age at the time," Helen Cooke explained to me, "but, when the reporters came and asked me how old I was, I always replied: 'Well, the Protest Committee says I am forty-six.'"

L. E.

CONTENTS

CONTENTS

PART ONE

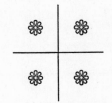

THE

ASSAULT

A MAN called Sylvester Gaffney wrote a ballad about the affair, when it was all over, and called it *The Battle of Baltinglass*. The ballad was published in Dublin, sold to the people of Eire, and sung—between deep draughts of velvet stout—in the public houses.

The words of the ballad did not always stick literally to the details of the events as they occurred, but no one quibbled about that. When Mr. Gaffney wrote that "there were Bren-guns and Sten-guns and whippet tanks galore" he undoubtedly borrowed from his imagination to suit his artistic purposes, for, indeed, the "whippet tanks" were four American-made squad cars, two station-wagons, and two trucks; but when he added that the battle was "raging up and down from pub to gen'ral store" he took nothing from and gave nothing to the truth.

Besides, there was none in Eire, by then, not fully conversant with the facts of the case; and the facts were incredible enough without quarrelling with Mr. Gaffney's fancy. For two months the newspapers of the country—and of other countries as far away as Australia in one direction and America in another—had given a blow-by-blow account of the battle, and even the blind had been able to follow the extraordinary events in braille.

Indeed, the slab of concrete in front of Cooke's Post Office in Baltinglass, over which the battle had raged, had been made as famous as that other stone in Blarney; and Miss Cooke had found herself an international figure.

Envelopes that had been sent through the private post-office run by the Helen Cooke Protest Committee and bearing the rubber-stamped words, in bright-red ink, BALTINGLASS DEMANDS CLEAN ADMINISTRATION, had been greedily snatched up by philatelists at home and abroad—and especially in that other island just across the Irish Sea—for their collections.

Tourists, including one well-known gentleman from Hollywood, U.S.A. (a reversal of the usual practice), drove miles out of their way to buy tuppenny-ha'penny stamps at the small, bright-green Government post-office in Baltinglass and take a good, gawking look at a small woman in her middle years, prematurely white, with a pretty face, a button nose, and light-blue eyes. They gazed at her as they would gaze at a king or a film star or an anteater in the zoo, and said to one another, in loud whispers: "But Miss Cooke doesn't look *anything* like her pictures in the paper, does she?"

As for the bizarre and heterogeneous elements that went to make up the battle itself; why, they have long since been transferred from the passing pages of the daily press into the folklore of the island, all mixed up with truth and fancy, with Deirdre, Sam MacAllister, Balor of the Evil Eye, Parnell, and the Little People. There, in that romantic mine, is the tale of the Baltinglass Air Force—though, to be truthful, it was but one small flying-machine (hired at that), piloted by a six-and-a-half-foot giant named Norman Ashe who was not from Baltinglass at all. He had taken a glider down, however, through screaming skies into Arnhem in 1944, and none would deny him his qualifications.

There, too, is the story of the terrible dawn, with the sleet biting down from a violent sky, when the Gardai arrived, all blue-uniformed and grim of purpose, to surprise the sleeping people of Baltinglass in their beds. And of how, thanks to the midnight ride of Bernie Sheridan and to the ringing of the auctioneer's handbell by Paddy O'Grady, the people of the village were ready for them instead and waiting, warlike, for the fray.

No; there was none who cared if Mr. Gaffney *had* taken a liberty or two with the truth, for the truth itself had taken liberties galore with the rules and the by-laws of ordinary existence. Who would have believed that the battle which had been caused by such a seeming trifle could have turned the whole country upside down—and then righted it again? Who would have credited that an affair concerning only an ailing old woman and her middle-aged niece could have inspired a few friends to stand in their defence, and after them most of the people of the village, and, after *them*, thousands on thousands up and down and across the entire Republic of Eire?

Of course, the fact that the Cooke family had run the Baltinglass Post Office for eighty years had some influence on the case and on the way the villagers felt about it; and when it was pointed out to Major-General Meade Edward Dennis that his grandfather, a district magistrate, had been instrumental in giving the original sub-postmastership to Michael Cooke in 1870—or thereabouts—he felt a certain responsibility towards Michael Cooke's granddaughter. The truth is that Cookes had been in charge so long that the building in Mill Street had been called Cooke's Post Office within the memory, even, of the oldest inhabitant. And in Eire a tradition is always a handy weapon to have, and to wield, in an argument.

There was another tradition involved in the fighting of the battle. The Protestant aristocracy of Eire, with their sympathy towards England and a related antipathy towards the intense nationalism of the Catholic majority, have rarely, perhaps never, previously participated on the side of the villagers in a village fight. By the time the battle was over this tradition had been shattered. Politics, religion, friendships, and feuds were forgotten in the fight for Helen Cooke: a sincere uprising by a democratic people against a Government that they thought had turned a blind eye to justice. As General Dennis put it: "This business has brought together a lot of the people in Baltinglass who would never, over the years, have grown to know one another so well; and it has helped us to see the strong points of one another." Or, in the blunter words of Helen Cooke herself: "We really had no use for Dennis or The O'Mahony until this happened. It was never known for folk of that class to take the part of the people before. Now the admiration for them is complete."

It was fortunate for Miss Cooke that the General came to her side, for, after all, few know as much of battles as generals do, and this particular one had had some excellent experience with big guns before— most recently with Field-Marshal Viscount Montgomery (an Irishman, too) in the Second World War. And she had other important supporters—including, it developed, a cousin of the Queen of England, who came to stand on the concrete slab; and another, called "The Pope," but not, however, the one in Rome; and many more, from both far and near.

Today, of course, peace belongs to Baltinglass, and the gentle ways of peace move its people. The River Slaney glides, a shining, polished sheet, along the pond above Joe Morrin's mill, and breaks excitedly over the weir and tumbles through the village. Tom Morrissey, a shop assistant in a hardware store, who knows the best places to find them, often fishes above and below the village for brown trout in the free waters; and the Major-General casts a fly elsewhere for the more aristocratic silver salmon; and the boys from Ben Hooper's Technical School stand on the Main Street bridge, an ancient, humpbacked arch, and break bits of bread into the water and watch other trout, grown fat and friendly, zoom to the surface and gulp them down. And Baltinglass Hill rises up over the village, steep and high, while on its grassy slope, at peace in his fresh grave, lies Father Doyle, who had written a letter to Mr. Costello, the Prime Minister of the Republic, on Helen Cooke's behalf, and had in his fashion fought valiantly for her too.

It is hard to believe now that the Battle of Baltinglass ever took place at all, except in the folklore of the magic island and in the lines of Mr. Gaffney's ballad—but it did.

It is important to note for later reference that Helen Cooke was born over the water, and to the north, and not in Eire at all. Her father, a Baltinglass boy—one of the ten children of Michael, the first Cooke sub-postmaster—had taken on a career as an excise officer. Since in the nineteenth century Ireland was part and parcel of the British Isles, his work had carried him to the big distilleries in Scotland, where he had married, and where—in Ardrishaig, Argyllshire—Helen greeted the world and was, as a matter of course, and owing to the religious beliefs of both her parents, baptized a daughter of the Roman Catholic Church. She was born strong-willed, quick-tempered, and intelligent; and, as the early years passed, her straw-coloured hair, seeming to borrow from the fire of her forming personality, took on an undertone of red.

While still a young girl, she moved with her family back to Ireland and, in the terrible twenties, when the Troubles were rife, identified herself with the militant Irish nationalists, acting as a messenger for an underground publishing venture. She took grave risks (for the punishment of such activities was not light), but few of her relatives knew of the part she played. Her qualities were many, and she could hold her tongue when the need was there.

In 1935 she went to Rathdrum, a village not many miles from Baltinglass, both being in County Wicklow, where she became acting sub-postmistress. One warm September day in the next year, when her future career seemed assured, she received an urgent letter, postmarked Baltinglass, from her aunt Katie Cooke, then sixty-eight. It contained the harsh, unwelcome news that an elder aunt, Bridget, the sub-postmistress, was ill with cancer. Family loyalty came high in the Cooke clan, and Helen, a forty-one-year-old spinster, pushed her personal ambitions behind her and left Rathdrum for Baltinglass to act as nurse. Bridget died three months later, and no sooner had she passed away than her eldest sister, Mary, aged eighty-three, fell and broke a hip. Helen stayed on to attend her needs, and, when Mary died, eleven weeks after Bridget, Aunt Katie, still the baby of the family at sixty-eight, was left alone. Pampered and petted always by her elders, Katie had scarcely learned in her long lifetime to mend her own stockings or to infuse her own tea. Helen sighed, unpacked her suitcases for good, and determined to devote herself to caring for the elderly, helpless woman.

Automatically, in the Cooke tradition, when Bridget died Aunt Katie asked for the sub-postmistress's position. The district postmaster at Naas thought this over for a while. Then he came to Baltinglass. "We won't be able to give the job to you," he told Aunt Katie, "since you appear to be over-age. But we could give it to your niece here in the morning." Aunt Katie's lower lip trembled, her spectacles, influenced by a spasm that crossed her face, took a little hop on her nose, and she was immersed in her own tears.

Helen came quickly to her defence.

"It's *her* job!" the younger woman told the postmaster from Naas, shaking a small, determined finger at his chin. "It's her job, and she's entitled to it, and I advise you to give it to her." She was a very small woman, but formidable when aflame, and, after all, the postmaster was only a man. He was, therefore, quick to recognize the hopelessness of his position. He agreed that, on second thought, Aunt Katie should get the job, over-age or no; but from the first it was Helen Cooke who did the work, kept the books, and wrote the letters.

In 1945 Aunt Katie had a stroke; and for a time she lost the use of her left hand and moved about with one foot dragging helplessly: but the business of the post-office went smoothly, capably on. She recovered within a year, much to her own pleased surprise, and then, in the spring of 1950, she suffered another attack. It was more serious this time. For a while she lay in her bed unconscious to the world. Later, when some thought returned, she was unable to see or to talk or to move her hands or feet; and still later, again to her happy surprise, she partially recovered. But, in April of that year, she resolved to resign as sub-postmistress, secure in her belief that Helen would take the position she was leaving and thus, with the small salary, maintain them both.

April passed, and May and June were over, and still there was no word that Helen Cooke's application had been favourably considered. At first there was no doubt in Helen's mind that she would be appointed; but as the weeks dragged slowly on and she did not hear, in spite of the confidence she felt, the suspense grew within her. She mentioned her embryonic fear to Father Patrick Doyle, the village priest, who wrote a recommendation on her behalf to the Minister for Posts and Telegraphs, Mr. James Everett. This was also signed by most of the shopkeepers of Baltinglass.

Helen Cooke was well and widely known; and, in addition to this recommendation, various others were sent in by community leaders. Deep inside her, Miss Cooke felt sure she would be named sub-postmistress when the time came. It was true that Michael Farrell, a handsome, sturdy young man of the village, had also applied for the job, but she was not really worried about him.

After all, she had had more than fourteen years of post-office experience now, and he had none. She was a Cooke, and there was the Cookes' post-office tradition to be kept up; and a Farrell could surely not do that. And, without the position, she could not keep her ailing aunt who had held the title—though not the reins—for so long; and, on the other hand, Farrell's father owned a drapery shop and a public house, and was well off according to Baltinglass standards. Surely, then, her case was the more deserving and the more meritorious.

But the weeks passed, and there was no sign from Naas or from Dublin. "Any word?" her Aunt Katie would ask, every so often. "Any word about it coming through, Nellie?"

"Not yet," Helen would reply, at first; and then, later: "Why, Aunt Katie, there's nothing to trouble yourself about. You're getting better, so I've just withdrawn your resignation." You see, she did not want her old aunt, now a frail and feeble eighty-two, to worry about the matter.

Once, in passing, she mentioned the subject to Bernie Sheridan, a young publican and baker, when he came to buy stamps. A forthright fellow, he laughed softly at her fears. "Don't worry about it, Miss Cooke. There isn't a man or woman in Baltinglass who believes you won't get the post." He turned to go, then faced her again, still smiling. "And if anything *should* happen you come to me. I happen to be a personal friend of General MacEoin, the Minister for Justice."

And that's the way it was all that summer, with Helen Cooke waiting, and, indeed, with young Michael Farrell waiting, for the appointment to come. September passed and October, and then at last, when it was least expected, the word came; the word, that is, which began the battle.

: 2 :

CON DEMPSEY, the district postmaster from Naas, is one of several who will remember that November afternoon deep into his old age. He had driven down to Baltinglass, a village in the Wicklow Mountains thirty-eight miles to the south of Dublin, to call on Helen Cooke. He stepped inside her little, well-kept bright-green post-office feeling uneasy in his errand, doubting his duty, and saw her, a tiny, shy-seeming woman of fifty-five, looking deceptively youthful in her faded working-smock, her cheeks pink and smooth, her eyes bright in their blueness.

He cleared his throat nervously, for Dempsey was a gentle man. "I want to speak to you privately, Miss Cooke," he said, with an eye on her three assistants. Then, in a cautious undertone, he added: "I've brought bad news."

Helen Cooke, allowing herself to show none of the anxiety she felt, led him into a back room. "Bad news? What is it?"

Dempsey plunged, taking his courage with him. "Michael Farrell has been appointed sub-postmaster of Baltinglass. I've been told to come and let you know." It was just three o'clock, and Dempsey took his leave, as quickly as he decently could, a few moments later.

That, then, was how it began. That was the delivery of the challenge of the powers that were in Dublin—though they, themselves, undoubtedly did not look on it as such, or as a springboard into trouble.

When at ten minutes past three Eileen O'Mahony, a girl in her twenties, came to buy stamps a shaken Miss Cooke asked her to carry her sad news to Father Doyle and to Father Moran, a village curate, both of whom had made it clear that they preferred her to Farrell for the job.

"It's more hurt I am than taken aback," she told Eileen. "It is the insult of being told, after fourteen years of slaving, that a man with no experience in the post-office whatever is more fitted for the job. And especially under the circumstances regarding my aunt."

It was just twenty-three minutes later that Benjamin Hooper stepped into the front door of his home. He was almost bowled over from behind by a whirlwind, caused by Felix O'Neill, a neighbour who lived across the Main Street.

"Did you hear, Ben?" O'Neill exclaimed breathlessly, and not stopping to apologize. "Michael Farrell has got the post-office!" O'Neill, a chunky man, with his pudgy face bracketed between an incipient double chin and a tangle of dark hair, was flushed rosy with excitement.

Hooper (and, indeed, the whole village) had known about Miss Cooke's application and about Michael Farrell's, and, like most of his neighbours, there had been no serious shadow of doubt in his mind that the appointment would go to the former. He was shocked into silence to learn that his calculations had gone astray. After the moment it took him to recover he asked: "What will become of the Cookes, Felix?" But O'Neill had already darted off like an eager, chubby gnome to spread the news. Soon all the village was buzzing with it.

Now, Ben Hooper was not a native of County Wicklow. Born in Cork, he had taken a job at the Baltinglass Technical School ten years before, and was now headmaster. A small man, with a fresh, pink skin, silken lashes over large and limpid eyes, with his head chronically, almost quizzically, tilted forward, and with a half-smile seeming to linger always just behind his lips, he resembled nothing more than a shy leprechaun. He hurried to consult his good friend Father Moran, a tall, slightly built priest.

"We've got to do something for Helen Cooke," Hooper said decisively, and the curate was quick to agree. But what?

The two pondered the problem, and presently Father Moran hesitantly suggested that they call a meeting of the vocational-educational committee of the school. Ben Farrell, Michael's father, was a member of the committee, and Father Moran was its chairman. "I could resign as a gesture of protest against the incident," the priest offered.

Hooper was doubtful about the idea. "Instead, why not make your protest at the Catholic Boy Scouts' Troop Committee meeting tonight? You're the chaplain, and both Mr. and Mrs. Farrell will be there and a number from the village." It was agreed, and, in fact, later followed through; but the effect of the protest was difficult to measure.

Thus, however, with deceptive tranquillity, began the Battle of Baltinglass, a wondrous affair that increased in volume and in a strange kind of violence until, later, when a deputy of the Dáil—Eire's parliament—spoke of the affair slightingly as "only a storm in a teacup," a Baltinglass man was able to retort with simple and telling truth: "It's grown into a damn big teacup and the tea is spilling out all over the country."

Yet, but for Bernard Sheridan, a husky, handsome, square-faced six-footer of thirty years, who had come to Baltinglass out of Eire's west five years before, it is possible that the battle might never have been fought. Baltinglass, with its eight hundred and more inhabitants, is in County Wicklow; and Wicklow men, they say, tend to mind their own affairs closely and are slowly wrought to anger. These, let it be made crystal clear, are not qualities of which to be ashamed.

But, in the west, a fight is jumped on quickly and made one's own.

:3:

I HAPPENED (Sheridan said) to be out shooting pheasant that afternoon with Teddy Graham on my brother-in-law's farm some miles from Baltinglass. It was on Thursday, the 23rd of November. Indeed, and I remember the day well, since I had shot four cock pheasants and had strayed off into the local priest's preserves by deliberate mistake and was then unfortunate enough to run smack into Father Mahar himself.

"Are you aware," he says to me, "that you are on my preserve?"

"Indeed and I'm sorry, Father," I say, and got off.

It was an overcast afternoon, cold but not quite freezing, and by five the light was too bad for shooting. We walked back to the car, Teddy and myself, and pulled up at Fanning's pub in Coolakenna, about ten miles from Baltinglass. We had two drinks of malt whisky to warm us up.

It was half past seven when I stepped inside my own door on the Main Street of Baltinglass.

My wife met me. Maureen is dark, and about my own age, and kind of pale in her colouring. She was excited; I could tell by the two touches of pink riding high on her cheeks.

"Bernie," she says, "Bernie, have you heard the news?"

"What news would that be?" I threw the four cock pheasants, just as they were, on the bar of my pub; and she passed no remark about my doing it, and then I was sure something terrible had happened.

"Miss Cooke has lost the post-office," she says, and a shiver ran through me, because this was the one thing happening I knew was impossible to happen. For, without the small income Helen Cooke would get from being postmistress, what would she and her old Aunt Katie have left to live on? Sure, I was well aware that Mick Farrell had also applied for the job, but there was no one in Baltinglass who believed

Helen Cooke would not be appointed, except for maybe Mick himself, and his father and mother.

"That's terrible," I says to Maureen. "It couldn't be." And all the good feel of being hunting and of the fresh air in my lungs and of the sweet weariness that comes from tramping through the woods was gone.

"It's a fact, Bernie, a true fact. Miss Cooke rang up, asking for you, and she told me. Aren't you going to do something about it? Aren't you going to phone her?"

"I can't at this exact moment," I says. "There's something has got to be done first, and I'm not sure what."

Then Maureen put her hand softly on my arm and she says: "Aren't you going to eat your dinner, Bernie?"

"I don't feel like my dinner," I says. And neither I did. I was hungry enough, coming in from the shooting and all, but what I'd just heard about Miss Cooke had filled up my appetite.

We had fried plaice for dinner that night, and I could only eat one small portion for thinking of what had happened. Those two unfortunate ladies would be destitute and out in the street—and what could I do to help?

I had known Nellie Cooke for the five years since I came to Baltinglass from Ballinalee. Running the post-office, she also ran the telephone service for the village. Her courtesy, efficiency, and friendliness over the phone had impressed me from the first.

Rigid in her fairness she was. If you were her best friend and asked for a priority over a firstcomer on the phone she would lose her temper at you; and she had one. "You'll just have to wait your turn like the rest," she'd snap. I was thinking of things like that, and trying to read the Dublin *Evening Herald*—but finding myself with the same line over and over again —when the phone rang at eight fifteen.

I yelled to Maureen. "If it's Miss Cooke say I'm out. Don't tell her I'm here."

I knew it was her; but I couldn't talk to her until I had some concrete plan in mind. I knew why she was coming to me, too: because I was acquainted with General Séan MacEoin, the Minister for Justice. You see, my uncle, who is now the Rev. James J. Sheridan, a parish priest in Fairchild, Wisconsin, the U.S.A., was the General's adjutant during the Troubles of the twenties.

Maureen told the lie for me. "Bernie isn't in, Miss Cooke," she says, blushing over the phone. "Can I take a message for him instead?"

"No, thank you," says Miss Cooke. "I'll ring again."

When Maureen hung up she turned to me and says: "Poor Miss Cooke, God help her. She's very much upset." She sounded as if she was not satisfied with the way I was not seeming to do anything about it; but I wanted to be able to lay a plan of action before Miss Cooke, and tell her what was going to be done. Sympathy alone was of no use. It would get her nowhere.

Indeed, I knew it was time to take some definite action to right the wrong. The first thing we've got to do, I says to myself, is to get the people together. To organize the village is the only hope. I took up the phone and called Soup Doyle, who is a publican like me.

"Have you heard the news?" I say.

"Yes—it's terrible." He knew right away what news I was talking about.

"Well, the Minister has made the appointment. Have you any ideas what we could do?"

"No, I haven't," Soup says.

"Will you help me, then, if I set about to form a committee?"

Soup coughed a little. "What kind of committee?"

"A protest committee."

"Mr. Sheridan," Soup says, suddenly very formal, "I have known Farrell's father quite a number of years. He is a very influential man; not the kind to meddle with."

I judged from this that Soup wasn't going to be helpful. "All right," I say, and hung up, wondering if this was going to be the reaction of all Baltinglass. The outlook seemed bleak for Helen Cooke and her old Aunt Katie. But I had to do something; I was wound up tight at the injustice of what had happened, and I had to act. I says to Maureen: "I've got nowhere there. I don't know what to do next, but I know one thing: I need some fresh air. I'm going out."

"Don't get yourself into any trouble," Maureen says, knowing me.

"Maybe I'll go and see the two county councillors, Paul Kehoe and Godfrey Timmons," I say.

I went up the Main Street and called first on Godfrey Timmons, who lives a quarter of a mile from my place. "Isn't this a terrible thing that has happened?" I say to him. He agreed with me. He is a publican and grocer, only a young lad of about twenty-two, of medium height, with a thin, sallow-complected face.

"The only thing we can do," he says, shaking his head from side to side, "is to get together and to set politics aside."

That is just what I wanted to hear. "Will you come with me, then, to see Paul Kehoe?"

"Why, yes," he says, "and delighted."

Paul is also a grocer and publican, and he lives just next door. He is forty, or thereabouts, and tall. He has brown hair, turning grey at the edges, and he is of a stocky build with a round face to go with it. We discussed the matter concerning Miss Cooke with him.

"Would you be prepared to come to Dublin with

me tomorrow," I say to him, "to see your Dáil representative, or any other Minister who would listen to reason?"

Paul Kehoe says: "That's a good idea, Bernie." And Godfrey Timmons nodded his agreement. Later Patrick O'Grady came round to call on Paul Kehoe. Paddy does clerical work and helps Joe O'Neill with his gasoline pumps. After a while Paul asked him if he would come up to Dublin with the rest of us. Paddy said, yes, he would, indeed.

I left them and walked round the village. It was a cold, blustery night, with ice in the puddles in the Main Street. The subject was being discussed at every bar in town—all sixteen of them. But there were no fights nor any violent arguments. The general opinion was that an injustice had been done. You could sense the gloom in the air.

I returned home at a little after nine and told Maureen about going to Dublin. "Timmons is going to see the organizer of the Fine Gael Party, and Kehoe is going to see somebody in the Fianna Fáil," I say. "He has nobody special in view. Paddy O'Grady is going to try for Seán MacBride, the Minister for External Affairs, and I am going to make a call on General MacEoin." The Fine Gael Party is the biggest party in the Government, which is a coalition with a small majority. The Fianna Fáil Party is the opposition, with Eamon de Valera at the head.

At ten in the evening I phoned Nellie Cooke.

"Hello, Miss Cooke," I say, very quickly, not letting her speak first. "I can't tell you how sorry I am to hear this; but I have some news for you. We are going to Dublin tomorrow about it."

Then she says: "I'm afraid it is too late, Mr. Sheridan."

She sounded broken down and beaten. I had never heard her like that before, for she has always been a woman of spirit.

"I'll come right down to see you," I say.

I went down. The town on the way was quiet; and it was very dark and getting colder. The earth of the Main Street crunched under my feet when I crossed it. I knocked on her door in Mill Street and she let me in, and I went, with her leading the way, into the cosy back-sitting-room, and there beside the fire was her old Aunt Katie. I saw that the old Miss Cooke had bloodshot eyes, as if she'd been crying all of the afternoon, and then I started to get more determined than ever I had been before.

Miss Katie made a feeble little smile at me. "I don't mind losing the post-office," she says. "It isn't really a job; it's a punishment, with the long hours and all. But at least we succeeded in keeping the home together with it."

I said nothing. What could I say?

Then a fresh tear came to Miss Katie's eye, and she says: "It's a nice thing now, in my old age, to see my home sold up after fifty years of service, and having to go off to England. I'm after having two strokes, and I'm afraid I'll never be able to manage it." This selling up and going to England was something new to me, and it came as a surprise. The scene was pathetic, and I didn't ask any questions about what Miss Katie had said.

"Where there's life, Miss Cooke, there's hope," I say, not able to think of anything original on the spur of the moment. "You haven't lost the post-office yet."

"Thank you," Miss Katie says. "But I don't think we'll be able to do anything now."

Without meaning to she was making it very hard. "Trust in God," I say. Then I told Nellie Cooke about our plans for Dublin, and she began to look hopeful, and supplied me with the information I'd need to put her case before the Minister for Justice. As I left for home she smiled at me.

"I hope you have luck, Mr. Sheridan," she says. And so did I.

:4:

THUS it was, next morning, that Bernard Sheridan with Godfrey Timmons, Paul Kehoe, and Patrick O'Grady drove to Dublin on Helen Cooke's behalf. They arrived in the grey, shabby, Georgian city at about half past eleven and then split forces to seek out their interviews. Sheridan went immediately to

General MacEoin's office in Leinster House, the home of the Dáil, and through the Minister's private secretary arranged to see him at three that afternoon. Then the thought struck him that he might find an ally for the Cooke cause in the offices of the *Sunday Press*. He made his way there. The chief reporter listened to him politely for half an hour, then asked: "But what can we do for you, Mr. Sheridan?"

"Why, we are wanting publicity for this case."

The chief reporter frowned. "I don't think you understand the position," he said. "It's very hard for us to give you publicity unless you people do something yourselves that would be newsworthy."

"I see," Sheridan said, thoughtfully. Then he left to meet the others at the Bedford van, owned by Timmons, in which they had come from Baltinglass. He met Kehoe on the way, and told him of his success in getting an appointment to see the Minister for Justice.

"I've had no such luck," Kehoe sighed. "I only met the Secretary of the Party, who said he'd put it before the executive council. I'm afraid, the way he sounded, nothing will come of it." The other two arrived at the van a few minutes later. It was now half past one in the afternoon.

"I didn't see MacBride," O'Grady admitted. "There's a Cabinet meeting this afternoon, and he's engaged."

Timmons chimed in. "I've seen my man," he said,

shrugging, "and he said why wasn't something done before now, and that we shouldn't have waited until the appointment was made. I told him the reason was that there was nothing we could do since the use of political influence would have disqualified Miss Cooke."

O'Grady, Timmons, and Kehoe turned to Sheridan. "It's up to you, then, Bernie, with the General," Timmons said. He didn't sound abundantly confident about Sheridan's prospects; and Sheridan, after the results of the other efforts, was beginning to doubt his own chances.

They had lunch then at a hotel, and afterwards proceeded, all together, to Leinster House again. While the other three waited in an antechamber Sheridan went in to see the Minister for Justice, a big, jovial-looking man with a red face and pure white hair brushed straight back. The Minister greeted him effusively and asked after his uncle in America. "When is he coming home? When did you last hear from him?" MacEoin asked. Sheridan told him. The cordiality of his reception had raised his hopes again. He cleared his throat, nervously.

"General," he said, "Miss Katie Cooke is running this post-office in Baltinglass for many years and has worked in it for fifty; and her niece, Miss Helen Cooke, is acting in the capacity of postmistress for her aunt for the past fourteen. This year, seven months ago, old Katie Cooke resigned through ill health, with the knowledge that the post-office would be carried on by her niece."

The Minister, listening, sucked in his cheeks, but said nothing.

Sheridan continued doggedly. "In all Governments prior to this one," he said, "the postmastership was handed on to the next of kin—provided, of course, they were living on the premises. It would almost look as if the regulations were made purposely to deprive Miss Cooke of her livelihood."

The face of the Minister for Justice purpled. "You don't mean to convey to me," he said coldly, "that you think a Minister would do a thing like that?"

"No, I wouldn't say that," Sheridan replied, "but a lot of people are going to *think* it. A lot of people are going to think it was all planned that way so that the job would go to Farrell."

For an awful moment it looked as if General MacEoin's temper had burst. Then, perhaps thinking of his birthplace in Ballinalee or of the days during the Troubles when Sheridan's uncle was his adjutant, his expression softened.

"Well, now, listen to me, sonny," he said, not unkindly. "Why in the name of God didn't you come to me forty-eight hours before this appointment was made, when there might have been something I could have been able to do about it? Now it's too late."

Sheridan now saw that his friendship with General MacEoin was not enough to swing him over; but he fought a stubborn rearguard action, hoping still to win his point or, at least, to ignore no opportunity. "Sir, it's never too late to right a wrong," he said. "And it's a glaring wrong, and it's a wrong that has got to be righted." Sheridan was a big-faced man, with a handsome, clean-cut profile, a wide forehead, a stub nose, and sunken eyes. His strong features were now as hard and determined as the famous Cliffs of Moher themselves.

"Be careful, sonny," MacEoin said. "I'd like to warn you at this stage not to get yourself into serious trouble in your eagerness."

"General, I'm thirty years of age, and I didn't come up here to be told that. I came to ask if you can do anything for us, even at this late hour."

The Minister shoved his chair back, and sighed. "Nothing can be done. The Minister for Posts and Telegraphs has made the appointment, and there is nothing you or I can do about it."

"Will you tell me one thing, then? Why was this appointment made three weeks ago, before Mr. Everett went to Strasbourg to preach there of human rights?"

MacEoin looked quickly up at Sheridan. "It wasn't. It couldn't have been or you'd have been notified in Baltinglass the next day."

"Yes, it was," Sheridan insisted quietly.

The Minister for Justice picked up his telephone. He got in touch with the private secretary of his colleague, the Minister for Posts and Telegraphs. Then, after a word with the private secretary, he set the phone back, very gently, in its cradle. "I'm very surprised," he said.

"Would you mind, General—I have three other men from Baltinglass waiting outside—would you ever mind receiving them and telling them what you've told me?"

"Not at all, sonny. Bring them in."

He rang for his secretary, and Kehoe, O'Grady, and Timmons were shown into his office, looking a little apprehensive. The Minister for Justice said to them: "I've been telling Sheridan that there's nothing you in Baltinglass, or I here, can do to help. The Minister has made the appointment, and whether he's right or whether he's wrong it's got to stay."

Sheridan pushed himself to his feet. "We're not going to stop, General, no matter what it costs. There's going to be a head-on collision between the people of Baltinglass and the powers that be; but we're going to have Miss Cooke reinstated in her rightful place in the post-office." Then he added anxiously: "We'll be no worse friends?"

"No. Certainly not." The older man was smiling.

Gloomy in their failure, the four Baltinglass men drove back to the village. "Well," O'Grady asked, "what's our next move, Bernie?"

Sheridan replied, with far more confidence than he felt: "There's only one thing for us to do now—form a committee of the people of Baltinglass. We've got to fight this thing tooth and nail."

When Sheridan arrived home Maureen had his dinner ready for him. He told her of his experiences in Dublin. Then he walked the quarter of a mile to the post-office to see Helen Cooke. He was feeling chastened now; and the weight of the forces arrayed against him seemed overwhelming. He told Helen Cooke of their unhappy efforts at Leinster House. Then he said: "Miss Cooke, you may lose the post-office, and if you do it may come as a shock to you. Be prepared for it. We'll do all in our power to prevent it." They settled down to discuss possible future moves, and presently the telephone rang and Helen answered it.

"It's Dublin, Mr. Sheridan, for you," she said.

The call was from Rory O'Connor, a reporter on the staff of the *Sunday Press*, who wanted to learn the details of the deputation to Dublin that day. Feeling that, at least, the visit to the capital had not been entirely wasted, Sheridan told the newspaperman what he wanted to know. Presently, improved a little in spirits, he walked back up the Main Street to his home, passing the statue of Sam MacAllister, a Scotsman who had been shot down in 1798 while trying to protect Michael Dwyer, a rebel leader. He had barely arrived when his own phone burred. It was O'Connor again, asking for more details of the post-office disagreement. "Also," the reporter requested, "can you tell me how to get an interview with Michael Farrell?"

"I'll arrange that for you," Sheridan promised. "Farrell has no phone, but you hold the line to Dublin open."

He hung up, rolled the exchange at Cooke's and asked to be connected to Webb's hardware store, next door to the Farrell establishment. Meanwhile he shot a quick word of warning along the wire to Dublin. "As soon as Farrell comes on and says 'hello' you cut in," he said to O'Connor.

The complicated switching of lines went through without a hitch, but Farrell refused to comment on the case. "I'll have my say later," he said. This was the first nibble of a press that at first seemed reluctant, but that later was to leap joyously upon the story and report its colourful findings to the people of the world.

: 5 :

PATRICK COGAN, a big, bluff deputy to the Dáil, lived in Tullow, a few miles to the south, and, since Baltinglass was on his route, he often passed through the village on his way to Dublin. He called in at Cooke's Post Office occasionally, and was well acquainted with Miss Helen. A long time ago—it now seemed—in June, he had begun to hear the buzzing of local gossip concerning the tardiness of the anticipated appointment, and, indeed, of how Michael Farrell had applied for the position, in open competition with Miss Cooke. Then, one day during the summer, Felix O'Neill had approached him to ask if he would lend himself towards making a representation to the Government in favour of Miss Cooke.

Cogan clapped O'Neill heartily on the back. "Why, Felix, there's very little need for that. The post-office in Baltinglass has such a good reputation, and the lady herself is so efficient, there is little likelihood that she won't be getting the job."

However, when Cogan chanced to run into the Minister for Posts and Telegraphs in the lobby of Leinster House a few days later, he brought up the Baltinglass complaint. Cogan had always got along well with Everett in the past, and he saw no reason why they should not continue to get along in the future. He had always voted on the same side as Everett in the House, even though he was himself an Independent Farmer and Everett was a Labour man, for they both supported the coalition Government.

To Cogan's surprise Everett confided that he had received some complaints about the way the Baltinglass Post Office was being run. Some letters, Everett said, had gone astray, according to his information. Cogan thanked the Minister, but was puzzled over the reported dissatisfaction. He had always found Helen Cooke, in his dealings with her, to be both helpful and efficient at her job.

The matter preyed on his mind during the following few days, and to rid himself of the irritant one morning he drove out of his way to call on Con Dempsey, the postmaster at Naas. "Have you had any complaints about the way the Baltinglass Post Office is being run?" Cogan asked. He said nothing about his conversation with Everett.

Dempsey laughed. "I regard Cooke's Post Office as the most efficient in my district," he said. "What, indeed, made you ask a thing like that?"

"Just idle curiosity," Cogan said innocently. He left the matter to rest there, assured that somewhere along the unavoidable tangle of official red tape a misunderstanding had cropped up, and feeling certain that it would straighten itself out in its own due course. He was not a man who believed in unnecessarily questioning Ministers of the Republic about appointments, and, in fact, considered it unfair to them to apply pressure that might hamper them in the course of their work. Then, on November 23, many months after the question had first nested in his mind, and when he had almost forgotten all about it, he received an urgent telephone-call from Helen Cooke herself.

"The other people got the post-office," she an-

nounced, sounding close to tears. "Is there not anything you can do?"

"Why, I'll try, Miss Cooke," Cogan promised, disturbed at the turn of events. "I'll surely try."

At once he requested an interview with John Costello, the Prime Minister. This, he felt, was an emergency, and in an emergency the best place to go was
to the top. He saw Costello on Friday, the same
afternoon that Sheridan, Kehoe, Timmons, and
O'Grady had come to Leinster House. Cogan out-
lined the facts of the Cooke case to the Taoiseach.

"I think surely something ought to be done about
it," he said earnestly, "before there is trouble in Baltinglass."

The Prime Minister, a dignified and handsome
man, allowed a dry smile to pass fleetingly over his
lips. Perhaps he thought this was—as it must indeed
have seemed—far too trivial a matter with which to
concern the elected leader of a nation. Perhaps, again,
he smiled at the utter ridiculousness of the idea that a
village as small and unimportant as Baltinglass could
cause trouble serious enough to sting his coalition
Government. Nevertheless, he assured Cogan that
he would discuss the matter with Mr. Everett, his
Minister for Posts and Telegraphs.

Mr. Cogan, for his own part, was not aware that
Bernard Sheridan and Benjamin Hooper, each on independent tacks and unknown to one another, were

making their first fumbling attempts to set the Cooke case right.

: 6 :

At half past five on the afternoon of Friday, November 24, Benjamin Hooper called on his friend Felix O'Neill, and found him bent over, sweating at his account books in the sitting-room of his home. O'Neill, delighted at the interruption, shoved his work aside and they talked about the hard and unkind blow that had hit Helen Cooke. At a quarter past six, while they were still on the subject, a purposeful Father Moran joined them. When he said: "I'd like you to do something for me if you would, Ben," the shy-seeming little schoolmaster rose at once and followed him out.

They climbed into the priest's black Austin and drove the short distance to Hooper's home, exchanging hardly a word. Gnawed by curiosity, and feeling that the priest was being unduly mysterious, Hooper nevertheless made no comment. They entered the house and made themselves comfortable before the living-room fire. Finally, after a gentle sigh, Father Moran broke his silence.

"I've made an appointment with Deputy Oliver Flanagan up in Mountmellick today," the curate said, in a low and purposely confidential tone. "I made it for between seven o'clock and half past seven tonight. Now, unfortunately, something else has come up which needs my attention, and I'll not after all be able to go myself. Can I ask you to go in my stead, Ben?" Flanagan, an Independent member, had won his seat in the last election with the largest poll in the country.

"Why, surely, Father. And what am I to see him about, then?"

"Why, indeed, about Miss Helen Cooke and the post-office. I will give you a letter of introduction so there will be no mistake."

Hooper showed him to a desk and provided paper and a pen. For a few minutes only the scratching of the nib and the faint, softly upward lapping of the broad blue flames from the coal fire in the grate broke the stillness. Presently Father Moran laid the pen down, blotted the letter, and passed it over to Hooper to read. When it was approved and handed back he folded it, folded it again and yet again, and slid it into an envelope.

"Good luck to you, Ben," he said, "for Miss Cooke's sake."

Hooper arrived in Flanagan's home in Mountmellick at a quarter past seven, in good time for the appointment. He cleared up the Deputy's puzzlement by handing him Father Moran's introductory letter. "The purpose of my visit," he said, getting down to cases at once, "is to ask for any assistance you could give us in trying to help to reinstate Miss Cooke." Hooper's words, stating the Baltinglass problem as he saw it, carried with them the soft, musical lilt of the south.

When he finished Flanagan shook his head. "I'm afraid I can't be helping you. You see, it was I who recommended Michael Farrell for the job. I want to tell you, here and now, how it happened." He paused.

"About five weeks back," he said, tapping his fingers nervously on the arm of his chair, "a cousin of mine, who is in charge of the Local Defence Forces for this district, wrote to me and asked if I could use my influence to have Michael Farrell, an L.D.F. officer, appointed to the postmastership of Baltinglass. I wrote back, appointing a date and hour in which I should meet Michael Farrell myself, personally, to see what sort of a man he was. He came, accompanied by my cousin, and told me of his service in the L.D.F., and also said he was grateful for my offer to see him. Before he left I promised to do my best for him.

"I called on the Minister for Posts and Telegraphs in the Dáil.

" 'I understand, Jim,' I said, 'that there is a vacancy for the position of postmaster in Baltinglass.'

" 'That is right,' said Jim.

"I recommended Farrell. I made strong representation to the Minister for Posts and Telegraphs on

his behalf, and eventually he appointed Michael Farrell to the job.

"I think you will agree, in the circumstances,"
Flanagan said, rising to his feet, "that I couldn't help
you at this stage. But if Father Moran had come to
me in time I might have made a similar recommendation in Miss Cooke's favour."

Just as Hooper was about to leave, the Deputy,
having accompanied him to the front door, said:
"Will you be seeing Paddy Cogan and Tim Brennan?" Cogan and Brennan were both deputies to the
Dáil, though on opposite sides of the House.

"Yes—probably I'll be seeing them tonight."

"Well, if you do, tell them the story exactly as I
told it to you."

Hooper left for the long, lonely drive back to
Baltinglass.

On Saturday morning at eleven o'clock a group of
Baltinglass businessmen—and others—who had been
called together by Bernie Sheridan and Felix O'Neill,
met in O'Neill's unused ice-cream parlour, next door
to his grocery shop. The ice-cream parlour, dazzling
with glass and chromium fittings and haphazardly
full of packing-cases—it was open for business only
in the summer—was crowded. The men there were
the nucleus of the Helen Cooke Protest Committee,
which was to be the General Staff for the battle yet

to come: Ben Hooper, John Doyle, Felix O'Neill, Luke McDonald, Paul Kehoe, Godfrey Timmons, Bill Judge, Sheridan, and one or two others. Until then Sheridan had known Hooper only to see and to nod to when they passed in the Main Street. There was no heating in the ice-cream parlour, and it was cold to the point of discomfort, but the men pushed up the collars of their overcoats and seemed not to notice.

After some desultory preliminary discussion it was moved, seconded, and then unanimously agreed to hold a public meeting of protest, against the injustice done Miss Cooke, in the Town Hall, a green-painted stone building facing the village square. The date set was Monday evening at eight o'clock. Ben Hooper suggested that Father Moran be asked to be chairman of the meeting. Somebody said that William Coventry, a local sign-painter, ought to be given the job of painting notices announcing the meeting. Then Sheridan came up with an offering. "I could drive up to Port Laoighise," he said, "and hire a public-address system from Tom O'Kelly. We could fasten one speaker inside the Town Hall and one outside, in case we have an overflow." Indeed, it was plain that Sheridan was a man who placed faith in modern mechanical devices. His suggestion was acclaimed, and the first meeting of the Helen Cooke Protest Committee broke up.

After lunch Sheridan drove the thirty miles to

Port Laoighise and picked up the public-address system, paying the two pounds rental fee for a five-day period out of his own pocket, a sum later refunded to him by public subscription, which also covered other expenses of the campaign. He fitted the loudspeaker and microphone to his Austin and drove back to Baltinglass, touring the streets of the village and the surrounding district.

Snow had fallen lightly the night before, and the roads were slippery for driving. There was the harassing nip of frost in the air, and a chill mist hung over the village. "This is Baltinglass calling!" he said, a call-signal that was to become as familiar as "good morning" in the weeks to come all over Eire. "A protest meeting in connection with the appointment of sub-postmaster in Baltinglass Post Office will be held on Monday, November 27, at 8 p.m." He repeated the message over and over again.

Meanwhile others were tacking up the notices Coventry had rushed through his paint shop: one, strategically, at the chapel gate, one in Kiltegan, a smaller village—with but two public houses compared to the sixteen in Baltinglass—four miles east of town, another in Rathvilly, to the south, and the fourth on a country road leading northward.

At three o'clock Hooper, with Bill Judge, his brother-in-law, called on Father Moran. Hooper repeated his conversation with Deputy Flanagan.

"Well," Judge commented, "if Flanagan was able

to get the post-office for Mick Farrell would there not be a hope he could get the Labour Exchange branch managership for Miss Cooke? At least it would be a living for her and her Aunt Katie."

Father Moran nodded quickly. "It might be worth trying, at that. I'll ask Father Doyle his opinion of it." The parish priest did not hesitate to agree, from his sick-bed, that the idea was worth pursuing. He had been ill with a serious heart-complaint for some months.

Thus blessed, Ben Hooper called on Helen Cooke. "Would you accept the branch managership if we got it?" he asked her.

"I'd rather take it than be jobless," she admitted. "And thank you indeed for trying."

Armed with Miss Cooke's approval, Father Moran lost no time in telephoning Oliver Flanagan. He fixed an appointment for seven that evening. The three—Judge, Hooper, and the curate—set out optimistically at half past five. They arrived at their destination shortly before seven, and at once shot a broadside at the Deputy, telling him he had done a bad job in helping Farrell, since by so doing he had put Miss Cooke and her ailing, aged aunt out into the street. Of course, they were not out in the street *yet*, but the three felt justified in anticipating an event that might easily take place in the near future, and they did not point out to Flanagan that they were looking ahead.

Flanagan shrugged. "I regret the circumstances. If I had known I would never have made the case for Michael Farrell. You should have come to me early on, Father Moran."

"What's past is past," Ben Hooper interjected quickly. "If you were so successful in getting the post-office for Mick Farrell perhaps you can still help us out."

Flanagan eyed him warily. "And how is that?"

"There is a vacancy for a branch managership in the Baltinglass Labour Exchange. If you can use the same influence to have Miss Cooke appointed to it as you did for Farrell at the post-office it would be a happy ending to what might've been a sad story. Otherwise we are sure the post-office appointment will lead to considerable trouble." Hooper went on to tell him of the plans being made in Baltinglass to voice the indignation of the people at the injustice done to Miss Cooke.

Flanagan, like the Prime Minister before him, was unimpressed. "And what can Baltinglass do?"

"Wait and see," Hooper said. Then he added: "If you can give us an assurance, right now this evening, that you will get the Labour Exchange for Miss Cooke we will guarantee that the preparations for a protest meeting in Baltinglass will be cut short."

Flanagan, still smiling, refused to commit himself. "I will try to get the Labour Exchange for Helen Cooke," he said. "I can make no promises."

On Sunday morning Bernie Sheridan drove his car, still equipped with the public-address attachment, to the village chapel. He pulled in to the shoulder of the road and parked. He waited there until Mass was over, and as the people of Baltinglass streamed out in white collars and pressed frocks, once again he earnestly announced the public protest-meeting for the following evening. That afternoon, still not content that he had saturated the district with news of the coming event, he carried the message first to Grangecon, a village five miles to the northeast, and then to Stratford-on-Slaney, three and a half miles upriver from Baltinglass. Later the Protest Committee met to make final preparations for what they hoped would be a big and successful meeting.

It was then that Ben Hooper brought disappointing news. He had asked Father Moran to act as chairman, but the curate had decided that he should not step that far beyond his clerical boundaries.

"In view of Father Moran not wishing to be chairman," Ben Hooper said, his head sloped forward as he stood in the midst of the group, "I suggest we ask General Dennis to take the chair. I understand he is with us in this thing." Major-General Meade Dennis, recently retired after years of gallant service in the British Army, lived in his ancestral home, Fortgranite House, three miles along the road towards Wicklow town.

"That's a good idea," Des Cullen, a chemist of the

village, agreed. He shuffled his cold feet on the un-
heated floor of O'Neill's ice-cream parlour.

"A *very* good idea," Sheridan said.

It was unanimously decided to adopt Hooper's
suggestion. Cullen was asked to approach the General with the request.

"I propose that we also invite The O'Mahony to
speak at this meeting," Felix O'Neill offered. The
O'Mahony, chief of all the O'Mahonys, was chairman of the Fine Gael Party in West Wicklow.
O'Neill, being secretary for the same group, had
sounded him out and found that he supported Miss
Cooke's cause. There was a quick, eager murmur of
approval. The O'Mahony was an important man, a
powerful man, and better indeed to have as a friend
than as a foe.

It was also decided, without a dissenting voice, to
ask Patrick Cogan, the Independent deputy who supported the Government, and Tim Brennan, a Fianna
Fáil deputy who lived near by, to speak at the meeting. There was no risk at all of refusal, for hadn't
both indicated their willingness well in advance?

The meeting broke up, leaving the members with
the satisfactory feeling that their preparations had
been well and truly made.

:7:

MAJOR-GENERAL MEADE DENNIS was in his fifties, but looked younger. Athletically slender, with a thin, quizzical face, he had always led an active, outdoor life, first in the British Army and now as a dairy farmer on his family estate, a rolling, wooded land, well watered and green. He had heard, months before, that Helen Cooke's appointment as sub-postmistress was long overdue, and now, at last, that Michael Farrell had been given the job. He was disturbed over the appointment, but was unable to decide, midst a maze of personal conflicts, whether or not to do anything concrete about it. Dennis was a member of the Protestant aristocracy—"a Cromwellian rancher," one of Farrell's supporters called him, stingingly, later—who traditionally kept clear of village skirmishes. For many years the viewpoint of his family and of his family's friends had not been precisely that of the Catholic village populace, though that is not to say he was a bad Irishman, since his conscience was always guided by what he considered to be best for his country. In addition, he was the direct landlord of the Farrells and the ground landlord of the Cookes, and he had nothing against either family. Perhaps he thought it would be wise to remain officially neutral, wherever his sympathies lay. Then, after the second meeting of the Helen Cooke Protest

Committee, Des Cullen telephoned him. Cullen told him of the public meeting planned for the following night.

"Will you take the chair?" Cullen asked him forthrightly.

The General, face to face now with his dilemma, hesitated. "I'll have to think about it," he said finally. "I can't give you an answer right now."

Not long after Dennis had thoughtfully hung up his telephone receiver Father Moran, looking pale and serious, drove up the gravel drive and parked his car in front of Fortgranite House—a cold and draughty seat. The General invited him into his study, and the two sat on the black-leather seats before a low, flickering fire that failed to make a deep impression on the large room. The curate indicated without preliminary that he was exceedingly upset over the development at the Baltinglass Post Office.

"Did you know," he said to Dennis, "that it was your grandfather who appointed Miss Cooke's grandfather as postmaster eighty years ago?"

It was a shrewd stroke, and the information took the General by surprise. "Why, no; I had no idea!"

"Indeed, and he did. I believe your grandfather's name was Meade Dennis, the same as yours. He said to Michael Cooke at the time: 'Now, Cooke,' he said, 'you have a very big family to keep. You may find some day that there's not enough food in your house for breakfast, and there's one thing I want to impress

upon you—never put your finger in the till.' Miss
Cooke tells me that that has been passed down in her
family as a tradition, in spirit and letter, for eighty
years."

It was at this point that Miss Cooke's cause suddenly struck Dennis in a new light—that of a family
responsibility. The curate went over the details of the
case with him again, and stressed how vital it was to
the success of Monday's meeting that he accept the
chairmanship.

"Of course," the General said. "I'll be glad to do
it."

Father Moran shook his hand heartily. "You won't
be regretting it," he declared. A moment later he was
gone.

Slowly, but very surely, the army of Cooke supporters was forming ranks.

: 8 :

BALTINGLASS (Sheridan said) is what you would
call a very conservative town. The people go about
their own business and don't mind anybody else's affairs. I was worried about it.

One of my regular customers, with a bottle of
stout before him, says to me just before Monday's
protest meeting at the Town Hall: "I'd like to see
you winning, Bernie," he says, "but you'll never suc-

ceed. When a Minister has spoken he has spoken. You're running right up against a stone wall, and I'm hoping your head is strong enough to take the blow."

"I know," I say, polishing the top of the bar, "but under the Constitution of Ireland we've a right to appeal to the President, and we will do it if necessary." I couldn't help wondering how many there were in Baltinglass who thought as he did.

Early Monday night I erected a loudspeaker outside the Town Hall—I'm by way of being mechanically inclined, and do all my own electrical work around the house. And as I worked at it I thought: "This speaker mustn't work if there's only a small attendance. It'd make us look like fools." Because of this, I fixed a switch that would turn the outside speaker off by a mere flick of the finger.

Then I waited. I was shaking with nerves: would the hall be empty or would it be filled to overflowing? We didn't know then how the town felt. And, at ten to eight that night, there were only fifteen people in the hall, including the speakers. The O'Mahony, unfortunately, had had a bad fall against a table in his own home at Grangecon and had broken three of his ribs, and would not be there. The palms of my hands were beginning to sweat, and it looked as if, very soon, I would have to go and find a hole and crawl into it and hide. The meeting was to begin at eight, but where was everybody? Maybe the people didn't care, I was thinking. I took up the mike and says through the outside speaker: "A meeting will take place here, in the Town Hall, in ten minutes' time."

I tried to make my voice sound steady, but I didn't feel that way at all.

Then the people started to move into the hall. At five minutes to eight it was half full, with about two hundred and fifty people, all standing except for the few in the ring of seats kept around the hall for the *ceilidhe*—the fortnightly social, you understand.

At three minutes to eight, feeling stronger, I spoke over the outside speaker again. "The meeting," I say, "is about to commence."

All at once the hall was packed. There were people there from the town itself and from the surrounding district. There were agricultural workers, still in their work clothes, shopkeepers, housewives, the twelve teachers, the two vets, and one of the doctors. There were six hundred inside the hall, and another hundred huddled in shop doorways around the square for protection against the cold mist, and listening to the speaker. It was indeed a lucky thing I had put it up.

General Dennis, as chairman, opened the meeting. "This meeting has been called to protest against a very great injustice," he says, "done to one of the most respected citizens of Baltinglass. We hope to get a mandate from the people to act on Miss Cooke's behalf. Neither politics nor religion enters into the mat-

ter at all. I feel very deeply about it personally, because my grandfather was instrumental in appointing
Miss Cooke's grandfather to be postmaster about
eighty years ago.

"It is not too late, even now, for Mr. Farrell to
withdraw his application, and, if he does, he will earn
the respect and appreciation of the whole of Baltinglass." The General paused and looked around at the
crowd, as if he was drumming an important message
home into their hearts. "Nobody," he says, "holds
any animosity towards him or his family."

Right then Patrick Green, one of Farrell's supporters, scrambled up on to the platform. "What
right have you to say you represent the people of
Baltinglass?" he says to the General, and it was loud
enough for all in the hall to hear. The General
looked at him. There wasn't a sound from anywhere.
Then the General turned to the crowd.

"Have I the right?" he says.

And, like one man, the crowd roared: "Yes!"

It was as if I had just begun to breathe for the first
time.

The General finished his opening speech and introduced Paddy Cogan, then Tim Brennan, and finally
Colonel Christopher Mitchell, who had come down
to represent The O'Mahony, housebound with his
broken ribs. They all spoke. Paul Kehoe rose to his
feet after them. "I propose that a protest about the
post-office appointment be sent to John Costello, the

Prime Minister, and to Seán T. O'Kelly, the President," he says, "and that copies be sent to the leaders of all political parties." This was passed.

The meeting ended with everyone feeling very happy and relieved, particularly myself. Now, especially because of the reaction to Paddy Green's interruption, we knew most of the town was behind us.

I took Deputy Cogan back to my pub, and we had a drink of sherry together to celebrate. But the only mention of the meeting in the press, apart from an account in the weekly Carlow *Nationalist*, was one inch in the *Irish Independent*, and that appeared on Wednesday, two days after the event. Indeed, it was peculiar that it took so long for people in certain quarters to wake up to what was taking place.

: 9 :

ITEM from the *Irish Press*, a Dublin morning newspaper, November 30:

POSTMISTRESS POSITION
IN CO. WICKLOW

At Question Time in the Dáil, yesterday, Mr Corish replying for the Minister for Posts and Telegraphs, told Mr P. Cogan (Ind.*) that there were two applicants for the vacancy of sub-post-

* Independent.

mistress at Baltinglass, created by the resignation of the previous holder on April 14 last. The appointment was conferred on Mr Michael T. Farrell, who was considered the most suitable candidate.

MR COGAN: Is the Parliamentary Secretary aware that the other applicant had thirteen years' satisfactory service in the Baltinglass Post Office, and had been acting Postmistress there for years, since the premises were transferred to her by her aunt?

Mr Corish said he was aware that the other applicant was working there, but she was not a Department employee. Suitability of premises, character and financial stability were taken into consideration, and it was considered that Mr Farrell was the most suitable candidate.

MR COGAN: Is the Parliamentary Secretary aware that the post-office was hitherto carried on exclusively in a premises where no other business was done, and that it has now been transferred to a public house which is the headquarters of the Minister's Party in Wicklow, and that the position has been given to the son of a county councillor of the Minister's party?

Mr T. Brennan (F.F.*) asked if the Parliamentary Secretary was aware of the high feeling of resentment obtaining in the area at the Minister's

* Fianna Fáil, the Opposition party.

action. In view of the fact that the position was in
one family for seventy to eighty years, and was
held by the lady herself for thirteen years, was it
necessary to change the regulations to give it to the
other applicant.

Mr Corish said he was not concerned about the
applicants' political affiliations. It was untrue to
say that the new post-office premises were in the
nature of a public house.

Mr Cogan said he would raise the matter on the
adjournment.

: 10 :

AT three o'clock on the afternoon of Thursday, November 30, a wave of excited indignation swept from
the crossroads at Mill Street and Main Street and
roared through the village. An engineer with a gang
of ten linesmen from the Department of Posts and
Telegraphs had arrived in Baltinglass, packed tightly
in a truck. They parked the truck outside Farrell's
drapery shop and public house and piled out, carrying pickaxes and shovels and bags of other tools. At
once they began to dig a trench, one foot wide by two
and a half feet deep and thirty yards long. The
trench led across Mill Street and up the Main Street
pavement into the Farrell shop at the point where
Michael Farrell's new post-office was to be located.

It was intended to carry the telephone cable into its future premises. The linesmen also installed a switchboard at Farrell's—a fifty-line board to replace the thirty-line one that had so long done duty at Cooke's —but they would still have to disconnect the cable leading into Cooke's before the new switchboard could be used.

Sheridan walked down to witness what was going on at a few minutes to four o'clock. He saw that villagers were walking past, pretending not to be aware of the Posts and Telegraphs workers, until Tom Morrissey, the assistant at Webb's hardware store, walked over to where the men were digging. He sniffed ostentatiously at the air.

"This place smells," Morrissey said in a carrying voice.

One of the workmen, looking up, snatched the bait. "What the hell do you mean?" he demanded.

Morrissey eyed him frigidly. "I mean you've cut in on a sewer," he said, and walked away.*

Feeling was now running high in the village. Here and there among the aroused townspeople an angry muttering could be heard. Caution was being left behind.

---

* Morrissey's remark later inspired Mr. Gaffney to write, as the fifth verse of his popular ballad:
The linesmen made a dash to open up the cable trench;
They opened up a sewer instead, Lord save us! What a stench!
A gentleman in jodhpurs swore: "By Jove! They're using gas!
The next will be an atom bomb on peaceful Baltinglass."

Because of his position as direct landlord of the Farrells and as ground landlord of the Cookes, Major-General Dennis had been hard put to make the decision to side with Helen Cooke, but he had made his decision, and now he was in the fight all the way. The O'Mahony had sent a telegram to the Prime Minister protesting against the Farrell appointment, and, since the chieftain was still in bed, the General decided to call on him to see if he had received a reply. He arrived in Grangecon at six o'clock. The O'Mahony, a man of strong opinions, had been a member of the Dáil as a colleague of Mr. Costello's from 1927 until 1938, but he had not yet had word from the Prime Minister.

A lean and cadaverous man with burning eyes, The O'Mahony blew up when Dennis told him of the laying of the new telephone cable that afternoon.

"If I was a fit man—pity I'm not—I'd go in there to Baltinglass and be arrested," he fumed. "It would make good reading in the Dublin papers tomorrow: THE O'MAHONY OF WICKLOW ARRESTED IN BALTINGLASS."

Pondering what The O'Mahony had said, and impressed by the potential value to the cause of press publicity, the General returned to report to the Protest Committee. The O'Mahony had given him an idea.

"Wouldn't it be a good thing," Dennis offered, "to have a picket on Cooke's Post Office and prevent the

linesmen from removing the cable or from disconnecting it from Cooke's?"

There was a quick murmur of approval.

"That picket," the General added, warming to the
subject, "must be prepared to be arrested if necessary. It would give us the publicity we sorely need."

Sheridan, who had been sitting on a packing-case—
the meeting was again being held in O'Neill's ice-
cream parlour—scrambled to his feet. "I'm prepared
to be arrested, General. Who else will come with
me?" He looked invitingly round at the others.

Paul Kehoe said quietly: "I'm with you, Bernie."

"Me too," Patrick O'Grady said. "Count me in on
it."

Ben Hooper stood up. "We're all willing to take
our turn, I expect. I'd suggest we put one lady on the
picket." The others nodded. John A. Doyle left the
meeting to approach Annie Jackson, a short, stout,
grey-haired publican with an establishment in Mill
Street.

"I'm ready whenever you need me," she told
Doyle, her round face alight.

Meanwhile Patrick O'Grady hurried round to
have Coventry rush through placards for the pickets
to carry. Next morning Miss Jackson, Sheridan,
O'Grady, and Kehoe marched up and down in front
of Cooke's. The placards they bore read: BALTIN-
GLASS DEMANDS JUSTICE: NO REMOVAL OF POST OF-
FICE, and BALTINGLASS DEMANDS CLEAN ADMINISTRA-

TION. People passing in the Dublin buses craned their necks at the picketers, wondering what was up. The few words thus far in the daily press had made no impact upon them.

But during the morning Sheridan, recalling that O'Connor of the *Sunday Press* had told him that the villagers themselves would "have to do something newsworthy," ducked into Miss Cooke's and telephoned the daily *Irish Press* in Dublin.

"There's a picket of townspeople on Cooke's Post Office today," he said to reporter Martin Fallon, a pink-faced, balding young man. "There may be arrests. Are you going to send some one down?" At two Fallon arrived, accompanied by a photographer. He was the lonely vanguard of newspapermen from Eire, Britain, and America who were soon to send the story of the battle to the far places of the earth.

During the afternoon a widow named Mrs. Kenna diffidently approached Sheridan as he picketed. "Can I help you in any way, Mr. Sheridan?" she asked.

"Well, now, Mrs. Kenna, and are you prepared to picket here in the cold and to be arrested if necessary?"

"I'll do anything to help this cause."

Sheridan jotted her name down on the back of a used envelope. Soon, very soon, the word spread all round the village, like oil on water, that volunteer pickets were needed. The people of the village queued up to Sheridan, men and women alike: Mary

O'Kelly, a publican's daughter, Michael Patterson, a butcher, Peadar Farrell, Father Doyle's chauffeur and handyman, and Mrs. William Burke, the wife of a publican, hurried to get their names on the roster; Maureen Sheridan, Jim Martin, Mrs. Joe O'Neill, Mrs. Seán O'Rafferty, and Joe Morrin, the miller, joined them. They were all eager to offer their services. By the day's end nearly fifty townsfolk had volunteered for duty.

At four in the afternoon two of the Government linesmen walked the hundred and fifty yards from Farrell's to Cooke's, carrying a heavy bag of tools. Patrick O'Grady, standing on the concrete slab that covered the cable connection, grinned uncertainly at John A. Doyle.

"Here they come," he said.

Doyle blocked the doorway leading into the Cooke Post Office with his burly frame, but the linesmen ignored his presence. Instead, they went to the slab.

O'Grady stood tensely on it, a slight man, with pale cheeks and dark eyes. He held his elbows in to his sides and his hands ready.

"What do you want?" he demanded.

"We'll be digging up this slab."

"You'll not!"

The nearest linesman snorted. He eyed O'Grady's slender figure significantly. "And who are you to stop us?"

"You'll take this slab up," O'Grady said, tight-lipped, "over my dead body."

"That goes for me, too," Doyle roared. He was a big man, six feet tall and built on generous lines. He looked what he was: a man of exceptional strength, and able to use it.

The second linesman had been silent. Now he plucked at his mate's sleeve.

"Come on away," he urged. "We're not going to mix it with them just yet." They retreated to Farrell's and reported to the engineer in charge. The very air seemed to crackle with undissipated tension.

As the two workmen hurried off Sheridan again slipped into Cooke's. He telephoned Major-General Dennis and told him of the latest development. About ten minutes later Dennis and his wife, a cheerfully plump woman, pulled up at the scene in their small estate-car.

"I'd like to go on picket duty right away," Mrs. Dennis volunteered.

She had hardly taken her position on the slab when McNulty, the Government engineer, a fair-haired, pipe-smoking man, approached her. He wore a trenchcoat and a tweed cap.

"Do you really think you're going to stop us from lifting the slab, Mrs. Dennis?" he asked.

She ran scornful eyes over him. "You'll have to have me moved by the police," she declared defiantly, "before you get me off this slab."

McNulty retired puzzled, shaking his head from side to side and muttering that he would telephone his headquarters in Waterford for instructions. In his job, a relatively straightforward one usually, he had never before been called upon to face such a problem as this. He put his call through to Waterford, but his superior there could suggest no way out of his dilemma. Waterford, in turn, telephoned national headquarters in Dublin, and was instructed to pull its men out of Baltinglass after they had finished their work at Farrell's. The rest would have to be abandoned, for the time being, and the problem would have to be examined with minute care before any positive action could be decided upon.

At six o'clock that evening, just before the linesmen left, Madame O'Mahony, the wife of the chieftain, turned up at the post-office and relieved Mrs. Dennis from her spell of duty on the slab. The O'Mahony's wife was an elderly woman, with a spare, delicately formed face. Some one hurried in to bring a rockingchair out from the Cooke house and placed it on the slab for her to sit upon. The evening had turned bitterly cold and, shortly before seven, one of the village women brought her a cup of steaming tea. She sat and drank it, rocking back and forth on the slab, and the people admired her for being there.

For a while during the day it had snowed, and the light fall had been packed down by the pickets until the pavement and road in front of Cooke's had become glazed and dangerously slippery. Presently, having observed the risk, Joe Morrin emerged from his mill across the street, carrying a bulging bag of wheat chaff, and scattered it on the icy surface of the road as a measure of insurance against falls.

The determined behavior of Mrs. Dennis, and the calm follow-up by Madame O'Mahony, both aristocrats, helped knit the village even more tightly together. With their husbands the two women had shattered an ancient precedent by standing and fighting side by side with the villagers and by helping them prevent the new post-office at Farrell's from opening on Government schedule.

There are some—such as Felix O'Neill—who consider this stand a vital one. "If the engineers had succeeded in moving us that first day," O'Neill said later, "I think we would have lost the battle. It was from that point that our publicity began to spread and gather momentum."

At eight that night the picket was withdrawn. Sheridan had earlier arranged a small but efficient espionage network among Baltinglass sympathizers in Government employ in Dublin, and word had come down from them that there would be no attempt that night to dig up the slab and disconnect the cable at Cooke's. To make assurance doubly sure Patrick O'Grady remained on duty that night so that he could warn the others should an unexpected move be made by Government forces. The night was moon-less and black, and growing even colder than it had been, but O'Grady made himself as comfortable as he could at the window of Joe Morrin's office, just opposite the post-office. A coal fire glowed at his feet, and there was a telephone ready at his elbow.

During the evening Sheridan, Dennis, and Joe Morrin, at the General's instigation, drove up to Dublin to call on Robert Smyllie, the editor of the *Irish Times,* a conservative and highly respected morning paper, in an effort to win his support. While General Dennis talked Smyllie listened, smoked his pipe, and now and then unconsciously twirled an end of his bold moustache. Outwardly, at least, he seemed unimpressed with Dennis's story.

Sheridan thought: "It's no use; he isn't sold on it. We are going to get the brush-off." Then, after twenty minutes of patient listening, Smyllie banged his fist on his desk-top.

"There *is* an injustice there," he said. "I'll have a man down in Baltinglass in the morning."

Next day the picketing recommenced. A reporter and a photographer came down from Dublin, as good as Smyllie's word, representing the *Irish Times.* At last the post-office disagreement was beginning to at-tract attention on a worthwhile scale. The initial newspaper-resistance seemed to have crumpled.

Meanwhile Miss Cooke had received instructions from an embarrassed district postal-headquarters to carry on for the Department until otherwise instructed. Since the telephone cable had not been transferred to Farrell's waiting switchboard, they had no alternative. The topic of conversation everywhere in the village—in the homes, on street corners, in the shops, and especially along the polished bars of the sixteen public houses—was of Miss Cooke and of young Mick Farrell and of the way the Department had been forced to back water and of what the Government would do next. There was a lull in the village, but it was a pregnant lull, weighted with expectancy and speculation, and with the promise of more and greater excitement to come.

Nor was the promise in any way to be broken.

: 11 :

SATURDAY, the 2nd of December, dawned quietly and died quietly; and there was no picketing on Sunday, although a cautious Patrick O'Grady looked in on the spot from time to time. Sheridan, enlarging the scope of his intelligence organization, had extended it to Carlow, fifteen miles to the west, where the linesmen had a sub-headquarters. A friend there watched and waited, and had promised to telephone him if they showed signs of starting out towards Baltinglass.

Sure, and all was peaceful; but in Dublin, at closed meetings, decisions for action were being made.

By Monday newspapermen, titillated by the skeleton reports of a mountain village standing brashly up against the Government of Eire, began to arrive from London. During the eventful week reporters and photographers streamed into Baltinglass from daily papers, weeklies, and the news agencies. The London office of *Life* sent a photographer, heavily equipped with cameras, flash bulbs, films, and instructions. Soon the telephone wires hummed with long messages, catching up on the colourful background, and in Australia, Canada, India, South Africa, the United States of America, and Britain the Cooke case was joyously spread out before newspaper readers. The editors rubbed their hands and waited for more, for here, in a dry spell, was an oasis of human interest, a story *of* the Common Man (or Woman) *for* the Common Man; but they did not consider, as editors don't, the discomforts and hardships of the men they had sent into the field for the story. Baltinglass was neither prepared nor equipped to accommodate the sudden influx of visitors from the press. There were a few rooms over the Ivy restaurant, it was true—rooms without central heating or citified conveniences; and the newspapermen, cursing the ups and downs of their calling, took them and pretended to smile.

Then, without fanfare, it was announced that on Wednesday Deputy Cogan would bring the matter up for discussion in the Dáil. For the people of Baltinglass, the news came like the call of a clarion. The village came aflame. The Protest Committee held an emergency meeting, and tentatively decided to put a picket of a dozen villagers on Leinster House, complete with placards announcing their grim allegiance to the Cooke cause.

On Tuesday Sheridan went to Dublin on private business, and bumped into a policeman friend.

"You needn't think of putting a picket on Leinster House, Bernie," the bluecoat cautioned. "It's illegal to picket the Dáil, and, besides, the Gardai have heard of your plans and intend to put a cordon around it to stop you."

"Thank you very much, pal," Sheridan said, thoughtfully. When he returned to Baltinglass he reported his encounter to General Dennis, and it was promptly agreed that it would be foolhardy to continue with the plan to picket the Dáil.

Then Sheridan said diffidently: "General, I have an idea. If it is illegal to picket Leinster House why can't we have a leaflet raid on it instead?"

"Eh, Sheridan? What do you mean, man?"

"Well, we could get leaflets printed and have them dropped on the people of Dublin, and on Leinster House in particular, by aeroplane. Wouldn't it make good reading the next morning to have the papers say that while Eire's police force guarded Leinster House the Baltinglass Protest Committee had struck from the air? Wouldn't it be fine, General?" Sheridan leaned forward in his eagerness, his face flushed and boyish.

The General nodded, pulling at his moustache. "It's a good idea." He rolled it over in his mind. "Yes, a first-rate idea."

"But, General," Sheridan said, "would you be having any idea as to how we'd get a plane?"

Dennis nodded. "Well, I think I have. There's a man in Dublin named Norman Ashe who has a plane. He was a glider pilot during the recent war, and has certainly got the spunk. I'm sure he'd do it for us. He has a photographic studio and specializes in aerial work. I'll get in touch with him right away."

Presently Dennis telephoned Sheridan. "I've been in touch with Norman Ashe," he said. "I'm afraid that plan we had won't work. It's against the law to drop anything from the air, and if Ashe did it for us they'd take his pilot's licence from him."

"That's too bad, General," Sheridan said, deeply disappointed.

"Don't give up entirely, Sheridan. There ought to be some way we can still use the idea."

"You mean you have something definite in mind?"

"Well, yes. Ashe tells me he has developed a new loudspeaker technique so that he can talk from the skies and be heard down on the ground. Perhaps we can get a message across that way, at a later date. It would be even more dramatic than dropping leaflets."

"Sure, it's too bad there'll be no time to work this out for tomorrow," the younger man said. "Perhaps we'd better forget all about it now, and keep it in mind for some future date."

"That would be best," Major-General Dennis said. "We'll keep it to ourselves until we can work something out."

Wednesday morning found the streets of the village seething with activity. Villagers crossed hurriedly from pavement to pavement, from door to door. In almost no time nine cars had been promised for the mass migration to Dublin, and a long list of villagers had indicated their eagerness to travel in them in order to be present for the anticipated fireworks in the Dáil. It was decided to limit each car to six passengers, and presently the honking convoy set out for the capital. Since it was evident that the Dáil could not be brought to Baltinglass, the villagers had elected to move Baltinglass, or a large slice of it, to the Dáil. Indeed, and they thought it would be a very great pity to miss the fun.

At six o'clock that evening—the affair was not due to come up in the Dáil until the adjournment at about half past ten—Sheridan, leaving no opportunity untested, called in at the editorial offices of the *Irish Independent*, the third of the Dublin morning papers, and a supporter of the Government. While talking to a reporter, he caught the word "Baltinglass" out of the corner of his eye on a page of typewritten copy resting on the newspaperman's desk-top.

By careful manœuvring he read the story while appearing to give his attention to the reporter. The typescript was an interview with the Garda in charge of the detachment assigned to Leinster House. "What will you do," a question in it read, "if Baltinglass puts a picket on Leinster House?" The policeman's answer was succinct. "I have my instructions. If a picket is attempted it will not pass through our cordon." Sheridan smiled inwardly. This time, at least, the Gardai would be disappointed, for Baltinglass had beaten them to the punch.

When he arrived at the Dáil Sheridan found that about a dozen villagers were waiting for him at the entrance. He wasted no time in sending word up to Deputy Cogan that they were there, and the Dáil representative came down at once and arranged for their admission to the public gallery.

"For God's sake, Bernie," Cogan warned earnestly, "don't let these people make any noise. It'll probably be noisy enough underneath, but whatever happens there you people keep yourselves under control."

Sheridan passed the word along. Then he gave Cogan a list of the remaining Baltinglass people who would be coming, so that tickets could be left at the entrance for them. That done, he made his way up to the public gallery and awaited developments. They were not long in coming.

: 12 :

ITEM from the front page of the *Irish Times*, a Dublin morning newspaper, December 7:

DÁIL UPROAR OVER DISPUTE IN BALTINGLASS

A large number of people from Baltinglass last night heard Mr Everett, Minister for Posts and Telegraphs, defend in the Dáil his decision to appoint Michael Farrell as postmaster.

The debate was one of the stormiest in the House for many years, and the Deputy Speaker called repeatedly for order.

The Minister was accused of "dirty, low-down, mean corruption," and at one period while he was answering a question on the subject, Mr Everett could not be heard for the remarks being shouted across the floor.

In reply to Mr P. Cogan, Indept. member for Wicklow, Mr Everett said that during the period in which Miss Cooke had been sub-postmistress at Baltinglass, there had been no serious complaint.

Mr Farrell, he said, was considered the most

suitable candidate according to qualifications. It was not the practice to give details of the evaluation of qualifications of candidates for such posts. Mr Farrell, he added, would take up duty as sub-postmaster as soon as the necessary arrangements were made.

"Is the Minister aware," asked Mr Cogan, "that the post-office has been in the hands of the Cooke family for over seventy years and that Miss Cooke has given fourteen years' satisfactory service in that post-office? And does the Minister think it fair to deprive a person of a position in which she has given fourteen years' satisfactory service to the Department and the local community, and to appoint a person who has no previous experience whatever, and who holds a licensed premises and other business?"

"I have given the Deputy full information," replied Mr Everett, adding: "Seventy years ago no other Irish person would have had an opportunity of applying for that job."

The Minister's remarks brought cries from the Opposition benches, and Mr T. Brennan (F.F.) asked what technical qualifications the proposed new postmaster had for the position.

"He is a member of the Labour Party," interjected Mr G. Boland (F.F.).

Mr Everett said that he would give his reply later in the evening.

"Why not give it now?" asked Mr P. Smith (F.F.).

When the Minister repeated that he would give his reply later, Mr Brennan said—"Don't be hedging."

"Does the Minister suggest," asked Mr Boland, "that the Cooke family are not nationalists? I can tell him that they have been nationalists since before the beginning of this century. They have always been nationalists."

"And no one knows that better than the Minister himself," suggested Mr Brennan. "The Minister has a long memory, sixteen years or so, and he is trying to get some of his own back now."

"It is nearly time," shouted a member of the Fine Gael bench.

While the Minister was reading his reply to the next question on the subject, his voice was almost drowned by remarks shouted from both sides of the House. He said that the estimated cost of transferring the equipment from the existing to the new post-office would be £146.

"Does the Minister consider it proper," asked Mr Brennan, "that public monies should be used in this way when they could better be utilised installing extra lines to help the overcharged system in that area?"

MR LEMASS (F.F.): The job has been done, and you are going to stick to it—isn't that it?

"It is dirty, low-down, mean corruption," shouted Mr. Smith.

In the evening, on the adjournment of the House, Mr Cogan said that he was not concerned with any change that had been made in the regulations concerning the appointment of a successor to Miss Katie Cooke, but he was concerned with the manner in which the appointment was made.

Political pull should not be the main consideration. Miss Helen Cooke had fourteen years' faithful service with the Department, and it was a contemptible quibble to suggest that she was not a direct employee of that Department.

"When I spoke to the Minister about this matter, he told me that there were some complaints against Miss Cooke, but he said today that there were no serious complaints.

"The Postmaster in Naas, who was in control of the post-office told me that there never had been any charge of irregularity of any kind, and that the post-office run by Miss Cooke was one of the most correctly run in the country."

These two defenceless women had now been ruthlessly deprived of their means of livelihood in order to make an appointment for a hanger-on of the Minister's Party.

Mr Cogan said that he challenged any member to go down to Baltinglass and say that Miss Cooke was not a good nationalist. She had done her duty in the Red Cross during the war, and the L.D.F was established to defend the country, not to attack a defenceless woman. The post-office was being transferred now to a public house which was not properly conducted.

MR McQUILLAN: On a point of order—

There was a chorus of cries from the Opposition benches, with booing and cat-calls and shouts to Mr McQuillan to sit down.

Further, Mr Cogan said that the man who had got the position had many opportunities of livelihood open to him without encroaching upon the living of two defenceless women. He had served in the L.D.F., but so did hundreds of others in the district. The issue was whether public positions should be given on merit or on the basis of "political corrpution." The appointment bore on its face all the marks of the brutality of Soviet rule.

Mr P. Little (F.F.), former Minister for Posts and Telegraphs, said that he would repudiate absolutely the suggestion that he had any responsibility in this matter. The regulation did not prevent the present Minister from appointing the niece of the postmistress.

Mr Everett, replying, said: "The difficulties which have arisen in filling the sub-postmastership of Baltinglass arise from a decision of mine in 1948. Some time after I became Minister for Posts and Telegraphs I instructed my Department that in future sub-post-offices should not be transferred to relatives except when the applicant was the husband, wife, son, daughter, brother, sister, widower or widow of the outgoing sub-postmaster."

Mr P. Smith (F.F.): You lied today at Question Time, so——

On both sides of the House uproar broke out, and the Deputy Speaker (Mr P. Hogan) asked Mr Smith to withdraw his statement.

Mr Smith: I will not withdraw that statement. He denied it at Question Time today. You (Mr Everett) lied against your predecessor today. You are a dirty, low-down rat.

Mr O. J. Flanagan (Ind.): If I go across you will——

In the general uproar the end of Mr Flanagan's statement could not be heard, and he was restrained from crossing the floor of the House by Mr Blowick, Minister for Lands.

Mr J. O'Leary (Lab.*): Take your medicine now. Take the answer now when you are getting it.

The House was in a turmoil at this stage, and it was impossible to distinguish what deputies were saying. The Deputy Speaker kept ringing the bell for order, and said that as Mr Smith had called the Minister a liar he would have to leave the House.

Mr Smith was attempting to speak, and the

* Labour Party.

Deputy Speaker said: "I want no explanation."

MR FLANAGAN: Send for the Guard.

DEPUTY SPEAKER: The Deputy must leave the House.

MR SMITH: It is time to have a show-down with you, too.

DEPUTY SPEAKER: I will name the Deputy.

MR SMITH: I do not care whether you do or not. You are a partisan and have been a partisan for the past three years. You are a political hack for the time you have been in that chair.

There were cries of "Shame" from the Government side of the House.

MR FLANAGAN: We will not stand for disrespect for the Chair.

MR EVERETT: He will not allow me to make a statement to clear the whole position.

The Deputy Speaker was endeavouring to be heard when Mr Smith shouted: "You have no right to name me, because you are not yet the Ceann Comhairle.* The Leas-Cheann Comhairle † has no right to name me."

Mr Flanagan again stepped from his seat and was restrained again by Mr Blowick.

CAPTAIN COWAN (Ind.): I move the adjournment.

MR SMITH (addressing the Deputy Speaker):

* The Speaker.
† The Deputy Speaker.

You are usurping the Chair's functions. You are a political hack and a partisan. We will expose you to the public as such.

MR SWEETMAN: You are only exposing yourself.

The Deputy Speaker, amid complete uproar, was heard to call for a vote on the question of whether Mr Smith should be named.

MR P. LITTLE (F.F.): On a point of order, can you take a vote after 10.30?

The Deputy Speaker then declared the House adjourned.

The Dáil will sit again at 10.30 a.m. today.

: 13 :

ALL this time (Sheridan said) while the fireworks was exploding down below us on the floor of the House the Baltinglass people were as impatient as caged wild lions behind the wire mesh that separates the public gallery from the rest of the Dáil. They gritted their teeth and, leaning as far forward as they could, curled their fingers around the wire, trying to keep quiet the way Paddy Cogan had warned.

Then I heard myself mumbling, and the good Lord up above knows I couldn't help myself. "That so-and-so Everett," I says, as well as certain other things, not knowing that the woman seated beside me was the wife of the gentleman concerned. Before I was aware of what was going on she had called a guard.

"That man," she says, pointing a stiff finger straight at me, "has been insulting a Minister. Put him out."

I was very much afraid that I would indeed be shown out of the House, for I did not wish to miss a word of what was happening down there. And perhaps I would have. But, as it happened, two of the Gardai from Baltinglass, Superintendent Heavey and Constable Dignam, had come up from the village and were standing right there in the public gallery with the other Gardai.

Tom Dignam hurried over, a scared look on his face. "For God's sake," he says, in a carrying whisper, "don't throw *that* one out. He's one of their leaders. If you put him out you'll have a real fuss on your hands." So, instead, they put me a few seats away from where I had been. I don't suppose you could blame Mrs. Everett at all for standing up for her husband the way she did—any Irishwoman would do the same.

When this happened it put the caution in me and made me mind myself more carefully; but the excitement was altogether too much for Des Cullen.

The next thing I knew he was yelling at the top of his lungs, so that even above the hubbub down below he could be heard, loud and clear. "Put Everett out!" he says. "Put him out!"

The Clerk of the Dáil, looking up with fury in his face, pointed a finger at Des and shouted to a guard: "Hold that man!"

And Des was taken away, protesting, and detained for a questioning that lasted an hour. Then, because he pleaded being ignorant to the etiquette of the Dáil, he was released with a caution. The way Des had behaved must have been a surprise to some because, you understand, he had been a personal friend of Everett himself, the Minister for Posts and Telegraphs having been a guest at Des's wedding some years before. It was becoming more and more clear that the Baltinglass affair was gathering momentum, and that it was a matter of principle with us. Now, in the taking of sides in the fight, the usual loyalties of friendships and the belonging to political parties didn't count any more.

After the Dáil broke up in disorder, I put through a telephone call to Baltinglass with the news of what had taken place, and then I went home with the others. All of us were feeling kind of pleased because of what had happened that night. It meant more publicity for the case.

Sure, and it did.

: 14 :

ON Thursday, December 7, Father Doyle, a white-haired invalid, too ill to guide a pen across paper himself, dictated to Ben Hooper a letter for the Prime Minister.

"I can foresee grave moral issues coming into the question," read the parish priest's letter.

> I am convinced that your Minister for Posts and Telegraphs has done a grave injustice in appointing Mr Farrell to the position which Miss Cooke so ably filled for so many years. I would be gratefully relieved if you would use your energies in bringing to a hasty conclusion the very unpleasant state of affairs now existing in Baltinglass. I have been ill for some considerable time, and now this nasty position is a great worry to me.
>
> I am with my people in their agitation, and I would be relieved if you would use your high office to see that the question is dealt with without delay.

The O'Mahony, also bedridden, the same day wrote to Mr. Costello threatening to resign as chairman of the West Wicklow Fine Gael Party, the chief Government party in the coalition. And that afternoon Mrs. Daphne Lalor, the wife of a farmer who lived two miles from Baltinglass, drove in to the post-office and sought out Bernie Sheridan.

"Is there not anything I can do to help, Mr. Sheridan?" she asked.

"Mrs. Lalor, certainly there is. You can picket and relieve some of those ladies so they can have a meal."

At half past one Mrs. Lalor took over Mrs. Kenna's place in the picket line, together with the placard she had been carrying. Sheridan moved across the street, in front of Joe Morrin's mill, to talk to Martin Fallon, one of the Dublin newspapermen. A Garda hurried over to them, hardly able to contain his excitement.

"Do you know who is picketing there now?" he demanded.

"Yes, it's Mrs. Lalor," Sheridan said.

"Ah, but are you aware of who she is?"

"Sure, she's the wife of a farmer up the road."

"No, that's not all. I hear she's a second cousin of the Queen of England. I'll find out for sure if you wish." He walked over to her.

Fallon turned eagerly to Sheridan. "Is this a joke, Mr. Sheridan? It's a bit cold for that." All round them villagers were stamping their feet on the frozen ground and blowing the cold off their fingers.

A moment later the Garda returned, grinning. "I'm right," he said. "She *is* a second cousin to the Queen of England."

"I wonder," Fallon said, hardly able to contain

himself, and looking round to make sure the other reporters were not within earshot, "I wonder would she give me an interview?"

"I'll ask her for you," the Garda volunteered. He did so, and Mrs. Lalor agreed.

"If you think an interview with me will help Miss Cooke," she said to Fallon, "you can have it. This is a grand cause to be out for. It is a matter of justice, and I'll stick behind it to the very end." At three o'clock that afternoon she was relieved from her spell of picketing and went home. Because of what later followed she made no further contribution to the Cooke cause.

Indeed, losing no time, supporters of husky Mick Farrell that very night held a torchlight procession up and down the Main Street. One placard they carried read: PEOPLE OF BALTINGLASS WANT NO RELATIONS WITH THE QUEEN OF ENGLAND. At a meeting in the Town Hall, after the parade, Quartermaster-Sergeant James Doyle, a close friend of the newly appointed sub-postmaster, said: "Farrell gave service to Ireland, whereas the relatives and supporters of Queen Elizabeth did not. Miss Cooke's supporters represent the remnants of British imperialism and royalty, which Farrell and many other decent Irishmen fought to put out." This was a reference to Farrell's service in the Home Guard of Eire, the L.D.F.; and it was evident that Doyle either did not know or chose to ignore the fact that Helen Cooke had been an active revolutionary against the British rule. The Farrell faction—outnumbered in Baltinglass, if not in the Dáil—were now fighting back fiercely with every weapon they could find. And, to try to counter-act the effect of the Helen Cooke Protest Committee, they had formed the Farrell Support Committee. Oh, and the two sides were battling back and forth, but largely in words and in actions that did not in-clude the use of the fist, the foot, nor yet of the shillelagh. Except, that is, for what happened at one o'clock that night between two of the reporters who had come from far away to write about the battle, and who shall remain nameless for the sake of them-selves, their wives, and their profession. They, in-deed, had been visiting in a purely social way around the various pubs of the town, and, returning to their rooms at the Ivy, found the front door locked—a not unusual thing at that time of the night.

There they were, then, with no key between the two of them, and—for reasons they could not later remember—it did not occur to either of them to knock on the door. Simple ways are sometimes hard-est to call upon, especially after an evening in the public houses, and, instead, they started an argument —which had nothing to do with Miss Cooke or with Mick Farrell—and the argument ended in blows, and somebody down the street, also returning from a series of social calls, yelled: "Fight! Fight! Fight!"

Then, in the dark and bitter night, there came the

complaint of windows opening, and the sight of bare heads and pyjamaed shoulders poking inquiringly out. And the people who looked and listened, the people who had heard the call, wondered at first: had the Battle of Baltinglass properly begun?

Some of them were relieved and some were not when they found out that it was, after all, only a private exchange of fists between two convivial gentlemen of the press.

: 15 :

EXTRACT from the Official Report, *Parliamentary Debates, Dáil Éireann*, December 7:

AN CEANN COMHAIRLE: The Leas-Cheann Comhairle.

AN LEAS-CHEANN COMHAIRLE: I desire to report to you that on the Adjournment Debate last night Deputy Patrick Smith, on being adjudged guilty of gross disorder by the Chair, was directed by the Chair to withdraw from the House. This he refused to do and continued to behave in a gross and disorderly manner necessitating the adjournment of the House without allowing the Minister who was in possession to be heard.

AN CEANN COMHAIRLE: I name Deputy Smith.

MR G. BOLAND: Is no one else to be named?

MR LEMASS: Has the Leas-Cheann Comhairle any other report to make to the Chair concerning disorder affecting any other Deputy?

THE TAOISEACH: I move that Deputy Smith be suspended from the service of the House.

MR SMITH: I beg to second that proposition.

MR LEMASS: I was not here myself last night but, according to Press reports and information given to me by other Deputies, there was a great deal of disorder—

AN CEANN COMHAIRLE: There was.

MR LEMASS: —in which a number of Deputies were concerned. It seems to me to be a dereliction of duty on the part of the Leas-Cheann Comhairle not to report any other Deputy.

MR MCGRATH: Is it not a fact that every effort was made to prevent Deputy Cogan from putting his case to the House?

AN CEANN COMHAIRLE: I am putting the question that Deputy Smith be suspended from the service of the House.

Question put.
The Dáil divided: Tá, 65; Níl, 47.
Question declared carried.
Deputy Smith withdrew from the Chamber.

MR LEMASS: May I point out that, according to reports in the Press, there was considerable disorder in the Dáil last night and apparently the

Leas-Cheann Comhairle is only taking notice of disorder on one side of the House?

AN CEANN COMHAIRLE: If the Leas-Cheann Comhairle is to be impeached, it must be done by a motion.

MR LEMASS: We will consider that, because there seems to me to have been a completely partisan administration by the Chair last night.

AN CEANN COMHAIRLE: The Minister was refused a hearing last night.

MR McGRATH: So was Deputy Cogan.

AN CEANN COMHAIRLE: The Chair is entitled to a hearing and the Minister did not get it. I propose that he gets ten minutes now.

MR SMITH (from the Lobby): The Minister lied last night. What about that?

A DEPUTY: Are you still there?

MR BRENNAN: May I point out, that I was interested in some of the questions dealing with this matter? Due to the attitude of some of the members on the Government Benches last night when Deputy Cogan was speaking, he could not finish—

MINISTER FOR EXTERNAL AFFAIRS (Mr Mac-Bride): On a point of order—

MR SMITH (from the Lobby): Listen to Pontius Pilate.

MR BRENNAN: He could not finish in time to allow me any time. May I press for time also to express my views clearly?

AN CEANN COMHAIRLE: Deputy Smith should leave the precincts of the House. By a vote of the House, his services have been dispensed with.

A DEPUTY: Go on, Pat.

A DEPUTY: He does not want to go now.

MR SMITH (from the Lobby): I am out of the House.

MINISTER FOR EXTERNAL AFFAIRS (Mr Mac-Bride): On a point of order—

AN CEANN COMHAIRLE: Deputy Smith must leave the precincts of the House.

MR McQUILLAN: Go on out.

MR SMITH (from the Lobby): You put me out.

AN CEANN COMHAIRLE: Deputy Smith has not left the precincts of the House.

MR McQUILLAN: Call the Sergeant-at-Arms.

MR G. BOLAND: I think the Chair knows its own business and needs no prompting.

AN CEANN COMHAIRLE: The Chair has stated that Deputy Smith must leave the precincts of the House. That is clear. He has not done so.

I adjourn the House for a quarter of an hour to give Deputy Smith a chance of obeying the ruling of the House.

The Dáil adjourned at 10.55 a.m. and resumed at 11.10 a.m.

: 16 :

FURTHER extract from the Official Report, *Parliamentary Debates, Dáil Éireann,* December 7:

AN CEANN COMHAIRLE: With reference to the excitement that arose in the debate last night in connection with the Baltinglass Post Office Appointment, a compromise solution, let us say, has been reached by permission of the House. Deputy Lemass will speak for five minutes and the Minister will have ten minutes in which to reply.

MR LEMASS: Before the Minister speaks on this Baltinglass affair, I think it is desirable to remind him and the House of the nature of the charge which has been made against him. In April last the postmistress of Baltinglass, Miss K. Cooke, resigned. She was an old lady whose health did not permit of her continuing the work of the office—the work having, in fact, been done for the previous fourteen years by her niece, Miss Helen Cooke, and done by her to the general public satisfaction. I understand that, in circumstances such as existed there, where a relative of the postmistress is available and qualified to carry on the work in the same premises, it has been the unfailing practice of the post-office not to advertise the vacancy, but to appoint the relative. In this particular case, however, the vacancy was advertised. It was assumed locally that the advertising of the vacancy was merely a formality and that inevitably Miss Helen Cooke would be appointed to the post. In consequence of that understanding, a number of people, who might otherwise have been candidates, either did not pursue their candidatures or withdrew them. Only one candidate sought the appointment in opposition to Miss Cooke, a Mr Michael Farrell. When it became known that there was opposition to the reappointment of Miss Cooke from that quarter, representations were made in favor of her appointment by representatives of every class and section in the area. Miss Cooke had, in the opinion of the people using the post-office, every qualification for the appointment. She was personally efficient and popular. She had fourteen years' experience in the working of the office. She had available to her, premises which were in use as the post-office in the area for some years and to which the telephone cables had recently been brought at considerable expense underground. She, as I said, had every possible qualification except one. She had no political pull.

The other candidate for the position was a Mr Michael Farrell, and he, so far as the views of the local inhabitants are concerned, had no qualifications for the office except one. He had a political pull. This Mr Michael Farrell is the son of a prominent supporter of the Minister in his own constituency. He was a member of the Minister's Party on the Wicklow County Council. He was selected by the Minister's Party, the National Labour Party, to contest the Kildare seat in the last general election against the present Minister for Social Welfare. He failed to do so by reason of the fact that he was two minutes late with his nomination paper. He has, in the views of the local people of all political opinions and all classes, no outstanding qualifications for the office. Let me say that in my view his political opinions and association with the Minister's Party is not necessarily a disqualification. The general view locally is that he is not a desirable person to be appointed. His father owns a public house. His father also owns a grocery business, a butchery business and a large drapery business in the town of Baltinglass.

A Deputy: More power to him.

Mr Lemass: There used to be a regulation in the Post Office which debarred the appointment to the position of postmaster or postmistress of any person who is concerned either directly or indirectly in the control or management of a licensed premises if other applicants had suitable premises available. I would be desirous of knowing from the Minister whether that regulation has also been amended or cancelled to permit of this appointment. The Minister has a choice between this person, whose father was a prominent and wealthy business man in the town of Baltinglass, and who was without experience or qualification, as against a lady who has no other form of livelihood, who had fourteen years' experience of the post and who was recommended by the great majority of the local interests which used the post-office.

I want to remove, if I may, the rather mean insinuation which the Minister attempted to make yesterday that the lady, Miss Cooke or her family, were in some way associated with the Castle tradition.* The Minister tried to justify his appointment on that insinuation. It is not a matter which concerns this issue. Even if the lady was not of the political opinions or religion of the majority, she would still be entitled to the appointment under the practice of the Department. But, in fact, the family have been for a long time intimately associated with the nationalist movement. On the face of it this looks like a discreditable political job. It is not merely a charge against the Minister. The Minister may have made a mistake. He may have been subjected to political pressure to make this appointment, but having made this appointment and having brought his Department into contempt it becomes a matter for the Government and not for the Minister. The Government cannot wash their hands of the blame in this matter by

* A reference to Dublin Castle, at one time the vice-regal seat. Hence implying antirepublicanism.

leaving it entirely to the Minister for Posts and Telegraphs.

MINISTER FOR POSTS AND TELEGRAPHS (Mr Everett): The difficulties which have arisen in filling the sub-postmastership of Baltinglass arise from a decision of mine in 1948. Some time after I became Minister for Posts and Telegraphs, I instructed my Department that, in future, sub-offices should not be transferred to relatives except when the applicant was the husband, wife, son, daughter, brother, sister, widower or widow of the outgoing sub-postmaster. Before that, sub-offices could be transferred at the option of the retiring sub-postmaster to a wider range of relatives. I saw, and see, no reason whatsoever why sub-postmaster-ships, unlike all other public appointments in the State, should be handed on by inheritance. I did not, however, make a complete break with the previous practice, as I felt it might be unfair to serving postmasters and, accordingly, I permitted transfer to immediate relatives. That decision was given by me in December, 1948, and I informed the sub-postmasters' union of it at an interview with them shortly afterwards.

Yesterday, I stated specifically at Question Time that it was I who had made this decision. My predecessor in office should be well aware, from his experience as Minister, that the application of the old regulations gave rise to grave difficulties.

Mr Little: I am not aware of it.

Mr Everett: The Deputy knew there was bargaining and that money passed between people.

Mr Little: I knew nothing of the sort.

Mr Everett: It must have come to the Deputy's knowledge.

Mr Little: There are difficulties, no matter what regulations one makes.

Mr Everett: A person could not transfer the postmastership unless someone was getting money from it and we were not in a position to say whether this was happening or not.

Mr Little: You were not forced to do it.

Mr Everett: The sub-postmistress of Baltinglass tendered her resignation on the 14th April last and accordingly the post was advertised. I should like to stress that this was done as a routine matter by my Department without any previous consultation with me. There were two candidates. One was Miss H. H. Cooke, the niece of the retiring sub-postmistress. She had been working in the office as assistant since 1936. The other candidate was Mr M. T. Farrell.

Both were good candidates. Miss Cooke has a satisfactory record as assistant and I do not wish to say anything which would appear to cast a reflection on her. The fact that she was an assistant confers no entitlement on her to appointment as sub-postmistress. Practically every day, and long before my time, assistants have been passed over in favor of other candidates. The strongest point, however, in Miss Cooke's favour, so far as I can judge from the arguments put forward, was that members of her family had held the office over a long period of years. It seems to be argued that she should, therefore, have been automatically appointed. My inclination, frankly, was in the opposite direction. This family has held the sub-office over a long period of years. Miss Cooke is not an immediate relative of the outgoing sub-postmistress and it did not seem unreasonable that the benefits of the employment should now go elsewhere in the event of another candidate, at least as good as Miss Cooke, offering. I consider Mr Farrell to be a better candidate.

MR BRENNAN: The people of Baltinglass do not think so.

MR EVERETT: On all the usual grounds of character, financial stability, etc., he is a good candidate. He is at least thirty years younger than the other candidate, he has had a college education and has given much voluntary service to his country. He became a lieutenant in the L.D.F. and Deputy Brennan was his district leader.

MR BRENNAN: I am giving him all credit for being a member of the L.D.F. There were several others as well as he.

MR EVERETT: In the L.D.F. days Deputy

Brennan was supporting a recruiting drive and promising that preference would be given to members of the Defence Forces seeking Government employment. This young man is still a member of the F.C.A.* and was highly recommended for the position of sub-postmaster by his commanding officer. I might mention that Mr Farrell was also recommended to the Department by at least four Fianna Fáil T.D.'s and Senators.

MR LEMASS: That was the deciding factor?

MR EVERETT: You cannot have it both ways. He was recommended by four prominent members of the Fianna Fáil Party.

MR LEMASS: Name them.

MR EVERETT: The Fianna Fáil Party is right, no matter what candidate is successful. They back both horses. I, however, had to take a decision as between these people and, on mature reflection, I regarded it as my duty to give the position to a person about whose qualifications I had no doubt whatsoever and who had served in his country's forces during the emergency. This step, I feel, will encourage other men in similar positions, and will let them see that the promises given to them on recruitment are not being broken.

I make no apology for giving preference to a young man like Mr Farrell, anxious to secure employment in this country, in preference to another

* *Forsa Cosanta Aitiul*, Gaelic for local defence force.

person who, while in no way personally objectionable, would, in the natural course of things, probably be retiring from office in another ten years or
so.

With the development, during this Government's term of office, of the various Post Office
services, particularly the telephone service, greatly
increased demands are being made on postmasters'
efficiency, and, bearing this in mind, I am anxious
that appointments to that class should be given to
active young people wherever it is reasonably
practicable to do so. Another motive which I have
in doing this is to give young men and women an
opportunity of making a home and a livelihood for
themselves in their own country. I do not agree
that because a grandmother has held a semi-Gov-
ernment job only her relations in this generation
have a right to the job, notwithstanding that other
citizens may have better qualifications. I was never
in favour of the closed trade policy which debars a
man from a living simply because his father had
not a similar one.

Reference has been made to the expenditure involved in changing the office from the present
building to the new one. Such expenditure is normal in practically every sub-office appointment and
while it could have been avoided had I selected
Miss Cooke, I would not be prepared to let that
consideration influence me in turning down a better

candidate. As Mr Farrell may be expected to hold the office for a long period the amount involved is a very small capital charge.

As regards representations made by the local people, I have considered these. I am not sure that they are altogether disinterested and I feel quite confident that, if the people in the Baltinglass area as a whole had an opportunity to make their wishes known in the matter, Mr Farrell would be supported by at least as strong a body of opinion as that which supports the other candidate.

According to the Official Debates . . . for last Wednesday, Deputy Cogan put the following question:

> Is the Minister aware that the business ha been transferred now to a public house, which has been the headquarters of the Minister's Party in West Wicklow and that the position has been given to the son of a county councillor, a member of the Minister's Party?

I wish to take this opportunity of making it clear to the House that the allegations in that question are incorrect. Mr Farrell's premises was not my Party's headquarters. All our meetings were held in the local cinema. Anyone who knows me knows also from my record that I am a bad supporter of the publicans. Again, it is not true to say that the position has been given to the son of a county councillor, a member of my Party. Mr Farrell, Senior, is not a member of the county council. At least, Deputy Cogan owes it to the House, if not to me, to give the facts of the case.

Mr Lemass: He was a councillor until the last election.

Mr Everett: I have no apology to offer for making the decision. I am taking full responsibility for it. The person was qualified and if Deputies require the names of the four Fianna Fáil representatives who supported him, they are Deputies Davern and Bob Ryan; Senators Andy Fogarty and S. Hayes.

Mr Lemass: On a point of privilege, is the Minister attempting to suggest that, in making appointments of this kind, he is influenced by recommendations from members of the Dáil or Seanad?

An Ceann Comhairle: That is not a point of privilege.

Mr Lemass: It does not make it any the less a dirty job.

An Ceann Comhairle: It is not a point of privilege on which the Deputy ostensibly rose.

Mr Cogan rose.

An Ceann Comhairle: I will not hear any more about the question.

: 17 :

MR. COSTELLO, the Prime Minister, was not at once aware of it, but that Friday was a black one for him (though certainly not so black as he was yet to face), for on that very day Paddy Cogan sat himself down in his home in Tullow, not many miles from the village of Baltinglass, and composed a letter.

"Dear Mr Costello," he wrote, taking his own time and making sure of his words,

Now that it is clear from the statement of Mr Everett in Dáil Éireann that the Government are supporting his action in depriving without justification a public servant of her only means of livelihood—

Mr. Cogan lifted his pen and paused to think—

I have decided, till this wrong is righted, that I will never again enter the division lobby on the Government side.

Mr. Cogan chewed the end of his pen, and stared through the wall of the room and through the snowy-sloped Wicklow Mountains into the infinite distance towards Dublin.

I feel that it is my duty as one of the Independent Deputies who supported your election to the office of Taoiseach to inform you of this decision, and to express the hope that a means shall be speedily found to undo this grave injustice.

I well appreciate that there are bigger issues involved than the filling of a minor post-office position. The civic conscience of plain people has been aroused by this grave injustice and the fight can go on. . . .

The Battle of Baltinglass is everybody's battle. It is a battle for clean administration and decent public life. It is a fight for justice for the weak and defenceless, and in particular in the exercise by a Minister of his executive functions.

I take this opportunity of thanking you for your unfailing courtesy and kindness to me, and sincerely hope you will find it possible to right this grave wrong.

Yours,
P. Cogan, T.D.

The Deputy read his letter over carefully, and then, satisfied, made copies of it to be sent to the daily Dublin newspapers so that there would be others, in addition to the Prime Minister, who would know exactly how Paddy Cogan stood in the matter of his vote in the Dáil and in the matter of Helen Cooke.

But, indeed, that was not the only message sent to Mr. Costello that day in connection with the Baltinglass affair. When the Rev. J. B. Fisher, the Rector of Kiltegan, a parish about four miles from Baltinglass, heard about how Father Doyle had sent a letter of protest to the Taoiseach he sat right down and wrote one himself, addressed to that same important personage.

"I have lived in the near vicinity of Baltinglass," said the reverend gentleman,

> for a number of years and have always found Miss Helen Cooke a very efficient postmistress. I would like to voice my strongest indignation at the action of the Minister for Posts and Telegraphs in changing the office without any apparent reason.
>
> In the interests of justice and good will I would appeal to you to effect an honourable settlement to this dispute, even at this late hour, and request the Minister himself to reconsider his decision.

Still another blow was struck that day (indirectly) against the Prime Minister and (directly) against the Prime Minister's Government.

At an evening meeting of the Helen Cooke Protest Committee—it was sometimes called the Baltinglass Protest Committee, but the Farrells objected to this all-embracing name—Bernie Sheridan suggested that the committee call off the picketing after Saturday. "Because," the husky, earnest young man said, "the Government could wear us out, having a considerable advantage in manpower."

Felix O'Neill agreed. After all, he pointed out, they had established their case. Now, perhaps, was the time to change their tactics.

The other committee members—Ben Hooper, the General, Des Cullen, and the rest—nodded. They saw the value of what O'Neill and Sheridan had said, and besides, lurking in the back of every mind was the uneasy thought that Christmas was fast approaching, and, with Christmas, the best shopping season in all the year, the shopping season that no Baltinglass merchant could afford to neglect, even for the sake of Helen Cooke. Indeed, and this was no slur on their willingness, for the merchants had already been giving freely of their time to the cause, with many of them spending more hours in aid of Miss Cooke than behind the counters of their shops; and they had also, and with equal generosity, been giving freely of the time of their willing shop-assistants. But now for a while, if regretfully, the balance would have to swing back to business.

Yes, it was unanimously agreed that the picketing would have to stop. But, on the other hand, they could not take the risk that the Government forces should attack and catch them wholly unprepared. What could be done? How to protect their businesses and the unprotected flank at the same time?

"I may be having an idea," Sheridan suggested diffidently, "which will get us out of this fix; and I would be glad to carry it through myself." He looked remarkably boyish as he continued: "I suggest an air-raid siren to be set up to warn the town."

"Eh?" said Felix O'Neill. "And what would we be needing with an air-raid signal?"

"I mean we could set up a couple of horns and sound them off to warn the whole town if the Gardai come. Then we would be ready to meet any kind of an attack."

It was agreed, without further argument or discussion, that this—combined with their espionage service —would be as effective a first line of defence as the picketing had been. Then the Committee moved on to other business, and finally the representatives of the press were called into the meeting—and eagerly anxious they were to be in on the news—so that a formal statement could be read out to them.

It was General Dennis who read the communiqué.

"We, the people of Baltinglass," the farmer-soldier said, "are now satisfied that we have established beyond all reasonable shadow of doubt that a grave injustice, which by now must be common knowledge, has been done by the Minister for Posts and Telegraphs. We deeply regret that the Government has endorsed the Minister's action.

"The matter now rests with those members of the Dáil who stand for integrity and clean administration. Baltinglass is one of many small towns, and what has happened to it may happen to your town tomorrow."

Thus, in the span of one day, the Prime Minister was attacked from three sides; but at the time it must have seemed to the great man like the attack of three mosquitoes, and ineffectual, stingless mosquitoes at that. For, in the high and secret places of Dublin, it had now been decided how to dispose of this awkward and embarrassing situation in Baltinglass—where there was a newly appointed sub-postmaster with his unused post-office, and, just down the street, a post-office that was still being used though it had no post-mistress in it.

And there was no doubt at all—in the high and secret places, that is—that very shortly Mr. Michael Farrell would be in and Miss Helen Cooke would be out, which would end the matter.

: 18 :

On Saturday morning (Sheridan said) I went to Patrick Dunne's garage at about half past eleven.

"Pat," I says, "have you got a couple of heavy horns so I can put them up as an air-raid siren?"

"Yes," Pat says, "I think I have just the thing." He went to the back of his garage and dug around in a greasy pile of cogs and axles and things like that. There was the banging and the scraping of metal against metal, and the smell of stale oil was stirred through the air. Soon he says: "Ah!" and came up out of the mess with the horns and handed them to me.

Pat had been a picket for Miss Cooke, and he was glad to lend the horns for the purpose I had in mind.

I took them home, and then I got to thinking. "These horns will be loud enough to warn the Main Street," I thought, "but what about the rest of Baltinglass?"

I walked down to Joe Morrin's place and found Joe there and say to him: "Joe," I say, pointing to the bell on top of his mill, the one that was once used for calling the millworkers to their jobs, "what about that old mill bell there? Can we ring it to warn the people in case of an attack?"

Joe says: "Oh, that bell? That bell is dangerous, Bernie; it may pull down the gable and all if we use it. The gable is very weak, and that is why we stopped using it."

"Oh," I say, disappointed. I looked at Joe, and then I looked up at the bell and the rope hanging down, and then I looked back at Joe Morrin. We stood there. He thought about it for a while, rubbing his chin. From the other side of the mill we could hear the water sliding over the millrace.

"I'll tell you what we'll do," Joe says finally, not rubbing his chin any more.

"Well, what?"

"We'll use it, and to hell with the danger of it and the gable coming down."

"Thanks, Joe," I say, slapping him on the shoulder, and I went off quickly to tell the press about the new arrangements: Joe Morrin's old mill bell would warn the Mill Street and the air-raid siren made out of Pat Dunne's horns would alarm the Main Street. And after I told the press, Jim McCann helped me put two horns up outside my bedroom window, and I fastened them to two twelve-volt batteries. Then we tested them. They worked fine, sounding sad and mournful, but fairly loud.

So the pickets were withdrawn, according to our plan, at seven o'clock that night. But, just to make certain that we wouldn't be taken by surprise in the meantime, Paddy O'Grady posted himself again in the office of Morrin's mill until ten that evening, with the coal fire flickering behind him and the telephone at his side, and with nothing to do except watch out of the window across the Mill Street to Cooke's Post Office.

That Saturday the stores and public houses in the town did a good trade, it being close to Christmas. And on Sunday, December the 10th it was, Mr. Ben Hooper, the headmaster of the Technical School, ran into some excitement of his own. In the Technical School Mr. Hooper runs a branch of the County Library, which he keeps open twice a week—Sundays and Wednesdays. He was there with his books when Miss Mary O'Kelly came in, excited. She is a pretty, fair-haired girl of about twenty-six, and she had come to borrow a book.

"Mr. Hooper," she says, "and did you ever see what is happening outside?"

"And what would that be?" Ben says.

"There are four men out there carrying placards against you. They are marching up and down where people are coming from St. Joseph's Church."

"Oh, indeed?" Ben Hooper says, acting as if it was no trouble to him at all.

Later in the day, when he left the Technical School, Mr. Hooper saw that the pickets were still marching up and down outside. The placards they were carrying said HOOPER MUST GO, and PARENTS: WITHDRAW YOUR CHILDREN FROM HOOPER'S CLASS, and again, IRISH WORKERS OF BALTINGLASS DEMAND REMOVAL OF HOOPER. Ben wasn't exactly pleased to read them.

That night I undressed for bed early, not much after eleven o'clock in the evening. It was about midnight when I heard a knock that came to the downstairs door. Our maid, Susie Byrne, a dark and pretty youngster, answered. She came up and tapped at our bedroom door and says, through it: "There's a man at the door to see you, Mr. Sheridan. He says it's important."

I went down, pulling a blue woollen dressing-gown on, and it was a friend of mine, a young man whose name I won't mention at this time. I can't say even now who he is because he was part of our secret service. "They're coming in the morning at seven thirty," he says, his voice shaking a little.

"*Who's* coming?" I say.

"The post-office engineers are coming, and the Gardai with them."

"Oh!" I say, with a funny feeling running through me like quicksilver, for the moment was at hand. This was the news from Dublin we had prepared for and were waiting for. "We'll have to hold a council of war," I say.

I dressed so fast it was amazing I didn't finish with both feet through the same trouser leg, and I went to call on Mr. Hooper, the headmaster of the Technical School, who lives just across the Main Street from me, and from him I called on Patrick O'Grady and then James McCann and then Felix O'Neill. I tried to wake up Paul Kehoe by knocking on his door, but Paul is a man who sleeps far from this world, and I had no luck.

"D-Day is in the morning at seven thirty," I say to each of the others. "We're holding an emergency meeting right away at my place. Tell the others."

All of them, excepting, of course, Paul Kehoe, got dressed and arrived at my place at twelve forty-five in the morning, and we met in the tap-room. I sent Patrick O'Grady to the post-office to awake Miss Cooke and to take over the switchboard and to connect all the switches—there was no night service then as there is now—and to give me a line to each subscriber as I asked for them. First I called John A. Doyle. It took five minutes for the ringing of the bell to waken him.

"It's tomorrow, John," I say. "They're coming at seven thirty."

"Oh, my God, Bernie, are you sure?" he says, sounding very wide awake for a man who was so recently asleep. He got dressed and came up here right away.

I phoned Mrs. Boreslaw Gaj—who is an Irish-woman, though married to a Pole—Mrs. Bellamy, Major George Anderson, Michael Patterson, Mrs. Joe O'Neill—in fact, all the subscribers in turn—and gave them the message to be in town and on hand for duty at seven thirty. "The Gardai and the linesmen are coming to disconnect the telephone cables from Miss Cooke's in the morning," I say. "They're coming in force. Be in town for it."

They all said they would be on hand at seven thirty.

Major Anderson lives five and a half miles out of town, to the northeast. He was half asleep or more when he answered the phone. He says: "When shall I be there, Mr. Sheridan?"

"About a quarter past seven, just to be certain sure," I say.

He looked down at his wrist-watch, which was pointing to twenty-five minutes to two. In his sleepy state he thought it was seven ten. It gave him quite a start, and he jumped into his clothes and into his car and hurried to my place as if the banshees were at his heels, and knocked at my door. I answered it, and, surprised at the quick sight of him, say: "Good morning, Major! I didn't mean for you to come right away."

"Why," he says, a little taken aback, "you said a quarter past seven." The major is a tall, middle-aged man with sandy hair and a red face.

"That's right," I say, "but that's tomorrow morning. It's not yet two."

He looked like a man with a puzzle on his mind. "Well," he says, "it was ten past seven when I left." Then he says: "Or at least I thought it was." A peculiar expression crept over his face, and he examined his watch closely.

"Oh, good Lord," he says, "I read the damn thing wrong!"

We had a drink together and he went home, his complexion healthier than when he came.

While I was making the calls the meeting was going on between the others at my place. In between getting the people on the phone and warning them of what was to come I listened to what was said, and offered my own suggestions. It was decided that John A. Doyle, Felix O'Neill, and myself would go out in Doyle's car—this was now a quarter past two o'clock in the morning—to Tuckmill, a crossroads two miles up the Dublin road.

We went, and woke up Ed Hanlon and his family, the widow of Charlie Short and her large family, and Joe Doyle and his family. They were all farmers. Then we went to Tom Moran's farm near by and woke the Morans up. "They're coming in the morning," I say. "Tell the neighbours." The word was spreading. We came back to Baltinglass and reported to the others, and the meeting was adjourned at three or a little after. I had no trouble falling asleep.

At six thirty I woke up. I had some corn flakes and a cup of tea. I didn't feel hungry, and my stomach felt nervy. Maureen says to me, putting a soft hand on my shoulder: "Be careful, Bernie. Don't get hurt."

"All right," I say.

As I was finishing my cup of tea Felix O'Neill, Jim McCann, and Paddy O'Grady came to pick me up, and I shoved the cup aside and left with them. O'Grady says: "What time will we set off the siren, Bernie?"

"At seven fifteen," I says. "That gives the people a quarter of an hour to get out of bed and dress."

At this point Paddy had an idea of his own, and he went to put it into action. He went to E. P. O'Kelly's place—O'Kelly is a grocer and auctioneer—with the intention of borrowing the bell O'Kelly uses for calling an auction. A big hand-bell it is. Mary O'Kelly was up and around when Paddy got there, and gave the bell to him after he told her why he wanted it.

Then, since she was up and getting impatient, she went to the post-office to be on hand when the Gardai and the engineers arrived.

The minutes were the slowest minutes I had ever waited for. At last seven fifteen came, and I went back to my place and threw the switch, and the siren started to wail, a mournful, drawn-out sound, like a dog bemoaning the moon. As soon as he heard it Paddy O'Grady started running around the town, clanging O'Kelly's hand-bell; a very good thing, too, because we couldn't get Joe Morrin out of bed to ring the bell in the mill, the way we had arranged it. Mr. Morrin is a very sound sleeper, and the mill bell was never used after all, but even at that it seems unlikely that the town of Baltinglass had ever before been awakened under similar circumstances or in such a clamour.

Oh, indeed, and the town woke up! When the siren died away and Paddy O'Grady stopped clanging at the hand-bell you could hear the sharp morning voices—excited voices—everywhere around. A baby cried somewhere near, and youngsters were shouting to one another as if it was Christmas morning, and I heard a woman's voice calling: "Don't get into any trouble now, Joe. Remember!" I couldn't make out which Joe it was or what he said in reply. I hurried down the Main Street and turned right along the Mill Street to Miss Cooke's.

Perhaps it was only a special awareness in me, but

it seemed as if the whole town was as taut as the high-
est fiddlestring. The minutes dragged. A crowd was
beginning to gather. When Major Anderson arrived
he grinned at me.

"This time," he says, "I got it right; eh, Mr. Sheridan?"

"Yes," I say, but I was watching the road for the
Gardai and the engineers. I was keeping my eyes on
the bend they would have to come round, and I was
tuning my ears in for the slightest sound of a motor
coming from that direction.

By seven forty they had not come. About eighty
people of the town were packed in the road in front
of Miss Cooke's, and others were arriving every minute in cars and vans from the outlying districts. Soon
there were more than a hundred. It was bitter, freezing cold. There was a driving sleet slanting into our
faces. Some of the people stamped their feet hard on
the ground and pulled up their coat collars. When
the picketing had started I had borrowed a street brazier from Carlow, about twelve miles away, and now
it was filled with orange-glowing coke, with the sleet
spluttering and arguing into it, and a circle of men
and women were huddled around it borrowing a little
of its warmth.

"Where are the Gardai, then?" somebody mut-
tered. "This is just a dress rehearsal that Bernie's
having."

I raised my voice. "Now, listen," I say, "I don't

want any of you people to think this is only a dress rehearsal. The enemy may be late, but he will be here shortly."

Meanwhile newcomers were arriving every minute. The General and Mrs. Dennis came at seven forty-seven, followed by Ben Hooper and Father O'Mahony, another Baltinglass curate. The General and, indeed, all of the Protest Committee, were afraid that if tempers flared up and fists flew—and maybe a few stones with them—the people of Baltinglass might get themselves badly hurt. The original idea, of course, had been to get someone arrested on the slab for the publicity it would bring. But now we were getting the publicity without the arrest, and there was no need to take chances.

General Dennis stood up on the pavement in front of the crowd. "Ladies and gentlemen," he says, "the Government have decided to enforce the Minister's decision. They are sending Gardai to Baltinglass, but we will have no violence. If they are determined to change the cable they'll succeed in doing it. We don't want any serious clash with authority."

There was a murmur running through the crowd, like a complaining wind, and I didn't care for the sound of it. Somebody made a funny, disbelieving snort. Miss Cooke and her sister, who had come from Roscommon to visit, began handing out cups of hot tea.

I kept watching the road, waiting, with a tight feeling in my throat. I was sure now that I heard motors in the distance, getting louder. At five minutes to eight somebody says in a high voice: "Here they come!"

It was the first of the police: two carloads of them and one radio car.

I forgot about the sleet and the cold, and, by the tense looks on their faces, so did everybody else. A moment later two trucks and more cars followed.

"Good God," a voice said behind me, "they're sending an entire army of men to do their job."

There were about seventy Gardai in all. The local superintendent of the Gardai, Tom Heavey, had gone up the road to meet them and came in with them. Chief Superintendent W. P. Quinn, from Bray, the head of the Gardai for all of County Wicklow, got out of the leading car, a big, stout, weather-beaten man, wearing a look of combined disappointment and surprise. He had good reason for this, and I could guess what was troubling him. He was wondering how it was that there should be a Baltinglass crowd to meet him and his army of men when the whole operation had been planned as a deep secret behind locked doors and, indeed, he had expected to find all of Baltinglass still snoring away in bed.

The crowd watched the Gardai, suspicious in their turn, and restless and waiting for action. It could not have been better timed if it had been planned when, at that precise moment, Soup Doyle charged into the crowd, waving a rusty old gun in his hands, a relic of the bad Troubles of 1798. There wasn't any shadow of a doubt now regarding his participation in the battle, and certainly none about the temper of the crowd. They were ready, and, in fact, some of them were anxious, to fight.

This, at last, was the showdown.

PART TWO

THE

DOGFIGHT

Soon after the early-morning descent of the police upon Baltinglass a team of post-office linesmen from Carlow and Waterford arrived, and parked their trucks outside the Farrell shop-cum-residence at the corner of Mill and Main streets. Their job was to disconnect the telephone cable leading into Helen Cooke's, and, while breaking the subscribers' service for as short a time as possible, to connect the new one into Farrell's. But the Cooke army stood fast on and around the concrete slab that covered the cable junction. As long as they remained there the linesmen could not carry out the instructions that had come down to them direct from an unaccustomedly high source. They were indeed in a quandary.

The police were similarly afflicted. Having anticipated a victory by default over a sleepy, unwarned village, and instead finding a belligerent reception-committee facing them, they now waited uneasily for fresh orders from Dublin. While they waited they walked aimlessly round the streets of Baltinglass in little groups, conscious of the hostility round them and wishing wholeheartedly that they were elsewhere on a less trying, less unpopular assignment. It seemed certain to them that they could not get the linesmen to the cable without a pitched battle, and that was the last thing they wanted.

Father O'Mahony, in the thick of the massed Cooke supporters round the slab, also felt the threatening cloud of violence. "What can I do to prevent it?" he thought. He pushed his way purposefully out of the crush and approached McNulty, the post-office engineer who was in charge of the linesmen.

"I am here," the curate said, "representing Father Doyle, who is ill and unable to be present. Father Doyle has written to the Taoiseach requesting him to reverse the decision of the Minister for Posts and Telegraphs. So far he has had no reply."

"Yes, Father?" the engineer said warily, waiting for the rest. He, too, seemed to be waiting for a solution without bloodshed.

"I was wondering," the curate continued tentatively, "if you could delay the execution of what you are supposed to do until Father Doyle receives a reply from the Prime Minister." He glanced significantly over his shoulder at the edgy Baltinglass battalion in front of the post-office.

McNulty sighed. "I'll do this much for you, Father," he said. "I'll telephone Dublin and give them the lay of the land and see what they have to say. More than that I cannot promise."

The engineer put through his call.

"Go ahead," he was told crisply. "Carry on with your instructions." He told Father O'Mahony that he would delay only until the arrival of the next post. He did so. And, indeed, at eleven o'clock a letter arrived for Father Doyle from the Prime Minister.

DEAR FATHER DOYLE,

I delayed replying to your letter of December 5 until the Minister for Posts and Telegraphs had an opportunity of making a statement in the Dáil on the matter to which your letter refers. Doubtless, you will have seen the report of his statement, which indicated that he had given full consideration to all relevant aspects of the appointment, including those to which your letter refers, before reaching a decision.

Yours sincerely,

J. A. COSTELLO

This obviously made no change in the situation. But, for a time, neither the engineers nor the police attempted a move. They appeared to be pinned down by the horns of their dilemma, worried and undecided. Meanwhile the supporters of Miss Cooke remained restlessly at their posts. They, too, had failed to envisage even a temporary stalemate. At half past ten the Protest Committee, meeting informally in the midst of the defenders and huddling for protection against the stinging sleet, decided to make one last attempt to reach Mick Farrell and persuade him to resign.

Accordingly General Dennis led a delegation composed of John Grogan, John A. Doyle, Bernie Sheridan, Tommy Doyle, and Luke McDonald up the Mill Street to Farrell's bar. As they entered they saw Ben Farrell, Mick's father, and a second later Mrs. Farrell, the mother of the newly appointed postmaster—a large woman with a determined jaw, her arms folded purposefully across her bosom—entered through an inside door.

"Good morning, gentlemen," she said, with steel in her voice. She was known round the town as a woman with a strong will; and, like many another mother, she was ambitious for her children.

Meade Dennis, being her landlord, knew Mrs. Farrell well. He said: "Could I have a quiet word with you, Mrs. Farrell?"

She nodded, and turned at once to lead the way upstairs into their living-quarters.

Dennis wasted no time in reaching the point. He explained what he had come for, and asked her to influence her son towards handing in his resignation at once. He was disappointed, though not precisely surprised, at her reply.

"I prefer death before dishonour," she said grandly, without seeming to recognize the staleness of her cliché. The words struck Dennis, a scholarly man, as being almost a parody of themselves. He looked at her to make sure that she was not pulling his leg, and saw that she was indeed quite serious.

"Then may I speak to Michael himself?" he asked.

"You may, General," Mrs. Farrell said, with formidable coolness, "but it will do you no good." She
called her son, and left the two men alone—Meade
Dennis, the lean, middle-aged aristocrat, and Michael Farrell, the chunkily built, ginger-haired, handsome young-man-about-town.

"Good morning, Michael," the General said.
"We've come to ask you to stand down at this late
hour. Will you do it?"

Young Farrell shook his head with sullen determination. "I don't care," he said, "if they shoot me. I
won't stand down. They knew I was an applicant, and
didn't ask me to stand down before."

Nevertheless, Dennis tried to dissuade him. For
the next quarter of an hour he kept at it.

"I want this job," Mick Farrell kept repeating.
But somehow the General gathered the impression
that he *would* withdraw his claim if given the opportunity to do so without losing too much face. Dennis had just formed this fleeting impression when
Farrell's father, a little, birdlike man with a tired
face, came upstairs and entered the room. He glanced
at his son appraisingly. "Ben has aged a great deal
lately," Dennis thought, feeling sorry for him.

Dennis said: "Ben, I've known you all my life. For
heaven's sake, man, climb down. This is going to
break you." He was convinced that if either parent
told the son to do so, he would resign.

Ben Farrell shook his head wearily. "If I was at the bottom of the pit," he declared, "I wouldn't climb down."

The General tried not to show how sorry he felt for the intense little man. He picked up the others in the bar and walked back with them along the Mill Street to where the Helen Cooke forces were still grimly emplaced round the concrete slab. He was keenly disappointed that the delegation had failed to move the Farrells to adopt a course of honourable surrender.

"I felt certain," he said later, "that we would win; and when we did it might leave the Farrells in an unenviable position with the people of Baltinglass."

: 2 :

THE engineers (Sheridan said) had been working at Farrell's, and the seventy Gardai were scattered around the town, walking around to keep themselves warm. It had cleared up, but it was still cold. Most of the people had gone home to have a belated breakfast, but a last-stand picket of seven or eight men and women remained at the post-office, including myself.

At one o'clock I saw the police assembling at Farrell's. I knew the time had come: I felt it in my bones. I rushed into Cooke's and got on the phone and told my wife: "Maureen," I say, "set off the siren, quick!"

Maureen rushed up, very excited, but she couldn't find the switch. My four-year-old son, who had been fooling with the wires and knew how it all worked, came into the room and threw the switch for her. The sirens wailed again, and the people poured out of their homes, still chewing on their food, and ran towards the post-office.

But by now the Gardai had formed cordons across the Mill Street, both above and below Cooke's. One of the Baltinglass men—I don't at this time recall who it was—walked right up against one of the cordons.

"Excuse me," he says, "but will you kindly let me through? You understand, I have to get back to my work."

The Gardai hadn't thought of that possibility, and, as they didn't have it in mind to block all normal traffic, they were very polite about it, and opened a gap big enough for him to go through. Of course, there were others who saw this work and decided to use the same idea. From both sides of the cordon about fifty of the people got through in twos and threes to "go to work," and gathered within the two bands of Gardai and again blocked the slab, standing on it and around it, and overflowing from the pavement into the road. Yes, I must admit that the Gardai were more than fair-minded about it all.

I could feel the mood of the people who had got through, and I didn't like it. They were anxious to get it over with, even if it meant a fight. I could feel that they were not in the mood to give in lightly. I was afraid they might look for violence, and some might get badly hurt; and now that publicity for Miss Cooke's case was ours for the asking there was no need to risk losing the sympathy of the rest of Ireland, which we wanted to keep, and which we might soon need.

"Ladies and gentlemen," I say, shouting it above their angry murmuring, "it is the expressed desire of the Protest Committee that we have no violence with authority." Some of them, who had not been there before to hear the General along the same lines, were indignant.

"Well, what did you want us here for?" somebody yelled from the crowd, and the rest of the people stirred like leaves under the influence of a wind, and you could hear them talking to one another, arguing and wondering, and, indeed, I didn't like the look of it. It seemed as if they'd forgotten what the General had said entirely.

"Simply and solely," I say, "for passive resistance. Simply and solely to show the world we fought a clean campaign!" There was a buzz all around me, and a resentful buzz it was, but the pressure towards a violent clash seemed to have lifted a little.

As if sensing the change in the crowd, the Gardai

chose that moment to go into action. They drove a truck, very slowly, along the edge of the pavement into the crowd; and we moved back in front of it, since there is very little a man on his own two feet can do to argue against a truck. There were a few scuffles between the one side and the other, and the glowing brazier of coke was tipped over in one of these, but no one was hurt and no arrests were made. We moved back stubbornly from the slab, and the Gardai, taking heart from the way the truck was succeeding, came along and helped it by grabbing some of us by the arms and encouraging us, using a certain amount of pressure, on our way. There was nothing we could do, short of using violence, and when it came to the crisis itself the people had listened to the General and to me and used passive resistance only. This was a very good thing for the long run, if not for the short. In a few minutes the Gardai were in possession of the slab itself.

It looked bad for us, just then, and there were those among the supporters of Miss Helen Cooke who felt for certain that we had lost the battle.

: 3 :

YES, there were many who thought the battle was over and done with and finished when the police, outnumbering the defenders within their twin, bracketing cordon, pushed them off and away from the slab. It did seem like final defeat, and certainly Miss Cooke thought it was, sighing, but nevertheless grateful to the hundreds who had tried to help her.

It was small consolation that the Gardai had used an unexpected weapon, the slowly driven truck employed almost as a tank, against which the Cooke army had no adequate defence. General Meade Dennis, with more experience in such matters, knew that the seeming success of the assault phase of an engagement between two opposing forces did not necessarily mean ultimate victory for the initiators of the attack. And some of the others, who knew nothing of military terms or military tactics, nevertheless refused to see surrender even when they and it stood toe to toe and face to face.

Why, even when the hour was at its blackest and the linesmen moved in on the concrete slab—so long inviolate—many of the defending army had not given up the fight. If they could not use violence, by direct order from their commanders, they could at least shout defiance to show that they had not fallen softly and without spirit, like ripe, surrendering apples to the pickers in an autumn orchard.

When the linesmen went to work on the cable they first erected a canvas hut over the concrete slab—almost, as was suggested from the crowd, as if they were ashamed of what they were doing.

"Are we in Russia," one of the Cooke men shouted with a certain amount of indignation, "or the Republic?"

"Put Everett out!" yelled another.

"Down with the police state!" said a third.

And all the while the police, fearing a counter-attack, encircled the busy linesmen and stood there ready to meet it.

When, at twelve forty-five, post-office linesmen prepared to work at their job of disconnecting the cable, Helen Cooke closed her front door and locked it with a bolt and chain.

"I was fuming," she said later, "at the right-is-might attitude of the powers-that-be."

A moment after she shot the bolt she heard a tapping at her front door. She swung the door open a few inches, to the limit of the chain, but she did not unfasten the bolt. "Yes?" she said. "Who is it?"

A man's voice replied that he was a newspaper reporter from London.

"And what would you be wanting?" Helen Cooke peered through the crack of the door.

"Oh, Miss Cooke," he said, "let me in!" He was a tall young man, warmly dressed. "My paper always phones me here at about one o'clock. Let me in!"

Miss Cooke thought it over. She had recognized the young man. He had always been polite to her, and his stories had been sympathetic to her and her cause. She hated to repay his sympathy with unkindness.

"Go round to the back," she whispered, "and climb over the garden wall."

He grinned his gratitude, and disappeared at once. She hurried out of her back door just in time to see him scrambling over the high stone wall and dropping down on the other side; just in time to see him landing in a puddle of melting sleet, teetering for a moment wildly, and falling on his back in the puddle. He was thoroughly soaked.

When he scrambled to his feet the reporter's grin was still there, if somewhat twisted. It was then that Miss Cooke belatedly discovered that she had neglected to bolt the side gate, which was swinging carelessly open. She thought it better not to point out to the newspaperman that he could just as easily have walked through on his own two feet and saved himself a wetting and a fall.

"Thank you very much, Miss Cooke," he said, "for your kindness."

Her smile was a little weak. "Come in and be taking your call. Hurry, now!"

Big-faced, easy-tongued Patrick Cogan, the Dáil deputy, had been attending a fair in Tullow when word came to him that the Gardai had descended on Baltinglass. He hurried at once to the battlefront, but arrived too late to see the taking of the concrete slab. The crowd of Cooke supporters were still gathered sullenly together, still now and then shouting defiance at their conquerors.

"Are you Irishmen at all?" they yelled at the linesmen. "Ireland is big enough: you could get another job!"

Cogan approached Sheridan and said to him: "I was at the fair in Tullow when I heard this, and came as fast as I could. What's to be done now?"

"I don't know," Sheridan replied unhappily. "I'm sure of only one thing. We've got to keep up the fight."

"Is there anything I can do to help?"

"Well," Sheridan said, "and if you'd get up and address the crowd and take their minds off the post-office it might be doing some good."

Cogan nodded. He was a good speaker, and he did not shy at the opportunity of addressing a ready-made audience. Somebody brought him a chair. Cogan stood up on it, and held out his beefy hands for silence.

"You are not fighting for Miss Cooke alone," he told the crowd, his voice booming out, "or the Cooke family, but for the people of Baltinglass. The Battle of Baltinglass is not over: it will go on!"

"Put Everett out!" a voice yelled from the crowd.

Cogan ignored the interruption. "The powers-that-be," he continued, "may for the moment overwhelm the people, but they will not trample them down as long as the spirit of freedom and justice lives in the town. Never again will it be possible for Ministers of any party to plot or plan in order to do injustice to decent people or to get favours for their friends."

When Cogan finished speaking he was followed by Reggie McCann and several others. This impromptu meeting lasted from shortly after two o'clock until about three. Then the crowd broke up and went quietly home. On their way they saw a group of eight Baltinglass women marching through the town carrying black flags of mourning, which they had hurriedly sewn together. By then, too, most of the village shops, except for the few whose proprietors were close friends of the Farrells, had drawn their blinds, as they customarily did for a funeral.

A group of Michael Farrell's jubilant supporters, about twenty-five of them, paraded up the Main Street carrying Eire's tricolour before them, certain of their victory. By four o'clock, however, a hush descended on the village. The sleet storm had long since passed, leaving a slight thaw behind it, and their failure to defend the concrete slab left the Cooke army feeling flat and empty, drained and dry. At seven that evening the new telephone cable was connected to Farrell's, and, with that, the Baltinglass Post Office was officially moved up the street to the corner of Mill and Main Streets.

That night post-office officials settled up accounts with Miss Cooke, and, when a postman arrived in Baltinglass with a bag full of mail from an outlying district, he was directed to Mick Farrell, the new sub-postmaster.

:4:

DURING the afternoon, soon after the cutting of the cable, Helen Cooke received a telegram from Leeds, in England. SORRY FOR BAD NEWS, it read, WE ARE ALWAYS HERE. It came from her brother and sister, Dr. Michael J. Cooke and Dr. Jessie N. Cooke, who were partners in medical practice. Coincidentally a Dublin reporter called to interview her a few minutes after she had read the message. As a result of this interview the following appeared in a front-page box of the *Irish Press* on December 12:

MISS COOKE TO SEEK WORK IN ENGLAND

Miss H. Cooke, the former acting postmistress in Baltinglass, told an *Irish Press* reporter that she intends to sell out and bring her aunt, Miss Katie Cooke, to England, where she will stay with her sisters and seek employment to enable her to support her aunt.

"Any employment I could secure in Baltinglass," she said, "would not enable me to support her, and if I were to open a business, I would only cut in on the livelihood of the people who aided me so wholeheartedly in the fight."

Indeed, it was true that at that stage Miss Cooke was ready to quit. Wasting no time, she even went so far as to put her house in the hands of local auction-eers for sale. But, before she could allow the sale to go through, General Dennis, who had heard of her decision to leave Baltinglass, hurried round to see her.

"Don't do it," he urged, his lean face anxious. "The people of Baltinglass won't allow you to go. If you did it would disgrace the country. If necessary a fund will be opened to support your aunt for the rest of her life."

"That's terribly kind of you, General," the little white-haired woman said, "but I can't accept that. I am perfectly willing and able to support my aunt. However, if you think it best, I'll reconsider going, at least for a while. I'm perfectly willing to remain here and see what develops." She was too proud to add that her savings were meagre and dwindling, and that the only way she could afford to remain would be to borrow from her brothers and sisters.

General Dennis, unaware of these circumstances, left with a feeling of great relief that she had, at least temporarily, changed her mind. For, with Miss

Cooke packed up and gone away, with her house sold behind her and her ties with Baltinglass severed, he knew that it would be impossible to continue the battle on her behalf. And if she remained . . . ?

He shook his greying head, worrying over it. If she remained—what? For, however he examined the situation, he could see that the odds against success were now very great indeed.

:5:

EXTRACT from the *Irish Times*, December 12:

Mr P. Cogan, T.D., who is supporting Miss Cooke, was at a fair in Tullow when he heard that Guards were being drafted into Baltinglass. He immediately went to Baltinglass where he learned that pickets supporting Mr Farrell were parading outside the technical school, protesting against the support given by Mr Hooper to Miss Cooke's cause. Mr Cogan sent a telegram to the Minister of Education protesting against the action of the picket, and urging the Minister to deal with the matter.

Ben Hooper was in his room at the Technical School that Monday morning when Tom Murphy, an assistant teacher, knocked at the door and entered. "There's a picket outside the school carrying placards," he said. He described the placards to Hooper. They were the same as before.

Hooper went on with his work as usual, but he could not refrain from glancing out at the pickets now and then. Their presence made him feel acutely uncomfortable, and he suspected strongly that the Farrell faction had picked on him since, as a public servant, he was the weakest link in the Cooke line of defence. He saw that at half past two they departed, taking their placards with them. To his immense relief they did not reappear the following day. The Dublin papers reported on Wednesday morning that the pickets had been withdrawn, but, as if to give them the lie, the pickets reappeared soon after the early editions had reached Baltinglass. When they came back on at the Technical School Ben Hooper, who could no longer conceal the disturbance he felt at their activity, rushed out to remonstrate with the picketers. He was surprised to find that this time they were not grown men but village schoolboys. In spite of his passionate objections they continued their backward and forward march in front of the school.

Hooper could not rid himself of the gnawing fear that, since he had stood up to be counted as an active Cooke supporter, the opposition was now trying to have him removed from his job. He had a wife and small children to keep, and he felt his responsibility to them strongly. Yet, at the same time, he felt in his heart that Miss Cooke had been treated unjustly, and he could not see himself, while remaining true to his principles, failing to continue actively on the Protest Committee. He was having a trying time.

Again, on Friday afternoon, two youthful picketers took up their post. Hooper could restrain himself no longer. He sent at once for the Gardai, and, when Guard McPartland arrived to question the picketers, the policeman learned that one of the youngsters, a lad named Curry, had been in school that forenoon, but had not returned to his classes after lunch. Mc-Partland scolded him for his truancy and escorted him back to school, whereupon the remaining pick-eter, unnerved by this show of authority, hurried away. To Hooper's great relief that ended the picket-ing against him.

"The Farrell Support Committee," Mick Farrell declared later, explaining the activities on his behalf, "was only an afterthought to kind of counteract the Protest Committee. They never did anything unless to counteract something done by the other crowd. Of course, after I was appointed sub-postmaster, I had to keep myself out of the firing-line."

: 6 :

NEITHER General Dennis nor Bernie Sheridan had allowed himself to forget Norman Ashe's suggestion that they hire his aeroplane, equipped with its public-address system, to broadcast for the Baltinglass cause. After the crushing defeat by the Gardai on Monday afternoon Sheridan had motored the seven miles to Castledermot to telephone Ashe ("I couldn't put a call through on Farrell's exchange," he explained later. "They'd know what I was talking about"), and learned that the ex-Arnhem glider-pilot charged twenty pounds an hour for the use of his specially equipped aircraft. Then, according to Sheridan, the following events occurred.

I reported this finding (Sheridan said) privately to General Dennis.

"I've been on the phone to Norman Ashe," I say to the General, "and he's prepared to do this job for us."

"That's a good idea," the General says. "We'll go ahead with that. We'll tell the others at the meeting."

We held a Protest Committee meeting that night at Felix O'Neill's. There was no talk of surrender. Indeed, it was admitted that the Government had won that day, but the members of the Committee, me included, agreed that this served to prove it wasn't an individual Minister of the Republic we were fighting any more, but the Government itself.

I got to my feet. "Our job," I say, "is to harass the Government when and where and however we can."

"Yes," Ben Hooper says.

When, following this, I suggested that a picket should be placed on the General Post Office in Dublin the others agreed that it would be a good idea to do so on Wednesday, when the Baltinglass question was to be brought once again to the attention of the Dáil. Fenton Doyle, Kitty Patterson, Sheila Hanlon, Felix O'Neill, Paddy and Tommy O'Grady, Lucy Doyle, and Jennie Byrne were to be the pickets. We decided that Paddy O'Grady would be in charge of the Dublin pickets and would arrange with Mr. Coventry for the placards to be made and lettered.

Then the General got up and told them about our plan to hire the aeroplane with the public-address system. It was received with unanimous approval. Then the General says: "I'll get a map now and see about his course and the likely time he'll be in the air." He reckoned the average speed would be ninety miles an hour.

After a few minutes' figuring he looks up and says: "I should say one and a half hours' flying-time would do it. The next question is," he says, "who will do the broadcasting?"

The General stopped and looked round the room, but no one says anything at all. Then the General says: "I'd suggest Sheridan. His voice suits the microphone, as we all found out at the Town Hall."

Everybody nodded and smiled at me: what could I do but nod and smile back?

Then the General says: "Now, at twenty pounds

an hour, this will cost us thirty pounds; and we have no more money. I'll give five pounds towards it myself."

Joe Morrin waved his hand. "I'll give five pounds," he says.

Felix O'Neill, Jim McCann, Luke McDonald, John A. Doyle, Paddy O'Neill, Mick Patterson, Tommy Morrissey, and myself—as well as some others I don't recall at this moment—we all pitched in and contributed, and in a few minutes the amount was oversubscribed by several pounds.

Then the Committee discussed the possibility of requesting subscribers to remove their phones as a gesture of protest against the Departments for Posts and Telegraphs.

"Why shouldn't we refuse to pay our telephone bills?" Des Cullen says. But no decision was reached on any action because we would have to get all the telephone subscribers and arrange a meeting in the Town Hall for the next night. We broke up the Protest Committee meeting at about a quarter past eleven.

Meanwhile the news that the Government had used a large force of special police to gain their ends in Baltinglass had spread all around the district, both near and far. At about half past ten the same night, four telephone poles were cut down by a cross-cut saw near Grangecon, taking with them the Dublin wires as they fell. In no time Baltinglass was buzzing with the details, except for the details of who it was who had done the cutting, because nobody knew that.

I could figure out what the idea behind the cutting was: it was for the psychological effect and not for the purpose of disconnecting Baltinglass completely from the outside world. Indeed, the doctors, the priests, and the Gardai could still route calls to Dublin or elsewhere through Tullow if they had any urgent messages.

The word of the cutting spread through the town as fast as rain. I was sure of one thing: the poles had not been cut down by townspeople, but by outside sympathizers with the Cooke cause. After they were cut, at about eleven thirty at night, a well-built, ruddy-faced man came into my public house and ordered a beer. He moved along the bar until he was opposite to where I was standing and says to me: "We've done a good job tonight for you."

I didn't know him at all, but a hunch came to me that he was connected with the cutting of the poles. "What was that?" I say.

He says: "We've cut down some poles."

Then I knew my hunch was correct, but my feeling was that, much as I appreciated the help and the spirit in which it was given, I couldn't show my appreciation nor could I encourage what had been done. It was grand, mind, to have it happen this once because of the psychological effect, but it had to stop there or it might become nationwide.

"And who gave you the authority to do that?" I say.

"Is that the way you're taking it?" he says, looking at me, surprised, and getting redder.

"I wouldn't be a party to any malicious damage or any vandalism."

He banged his beer down on the bar. "I'll go where I get more encouragement," he says, and walked out in a black huff.

:7:

On Tuesday the Cooke supporters, refusing on principle to patronize Michael Farrell, organized their own private post-office. Mail was left at Felix O'Neill's, who was licensed to sell postage-stamps, and a duty roster was drawn up for collecting it and posting it in the neighbouring villages of Grangecon and Rathvilly. Ben Hooper, the Technical School's headmaster, was at the top of the roster. The picketing directed against him had not shaken his determination to help Miss Cooke to the end. He loaded his small car with letters and parcels. Christmas was approaching fast, and his back seat was piled high with wrapped-up turkeys and other food-offerings to villagers' friends and relatives who lived in austerity Britain.

Next day Soup Doyle took over, and so on down the line, through William Burke and Mick Patterson, Father James Moran and Peadar Farrell (Father Doyle's handyman and chauffeur, who represented the parish priest in this venture), and down the long list of volunteers. The Protest Committee invested some of its subscribed funds in the purchase of a rubber stamp and a pad of red ink. The stamp said BALTINGLASS DEMANDS CLEAN ADMINISTRATION, and every letter posted by a Cooke supporter welcomed its bold imprint. Even the paper money leaving Baltinglass wore the message, which, by now, was being spread by every means available. Meanwhile letters of sympathy and encouragement were already pouring in to Miss Cooke, that courageous little woman who seemed to appeal to distant imaginations —messages now from Eire and Britain, across the narrow sea, and later from the far-flung Dominions and from places like Boston and Chicago and Philadelphia, in the United States of America, where, it seemed, there was many a good Irishman who could appreciate a brave fight against odds. And all across the Irish nation, now, many thousands who had followed the doings of the Protest Committee were beginning to pick up the Cooke cause and make it their own. These letters, being incoming and not outgoing, were no concern of the private post-office of the Cooke army, and, instead, were delivered to

Miss Cooke from the Farrell Post Office, but nobody at the time was interested in pointing out the irony of it all.

It was on Tuesday night that the meeting of the telephone subscribers was held in the Town Hall. J. R. Grogan, of Slaney Park, on the eastern side of Baltinglass, was elected chairman of the telephone-subscribers' committee, and explained why they had been called together.

"The object of this meeting," he said, "is to examine the best means of dealing with this telephone situation now that Miss Cooke has lost the exchange, together with her post-office. Shall we have our telephones removed—or not? Shall we use them—or not?" Grogan was a tall, quiet-spoken, middle-aged man. "If any of you have any suggestions to offer please stand up."

Des Cullen, a pale, thickset young man, rose to his feet. "I feel strongly that we should remove our telephones." He sat down again.

Frank Richmond, the general manager of R. N. Gillespie, Ltd., hardware merchants, jumped up, apparently agitated at Cullen's suggestion.

"Why cut off our nose to spite our face?" he demanded. "What would we do without our phones? I don't mind doing without if it will do some good; but I think if we remove them it will only mean Farrell will need one employee less to operate his switchboard. It will be playing right into his hands. I suggest that instead of removing our phones we use them more than ever, at all times, to inquire the time, anything. And this will add to the amount of confusion that already exists at Farrell's."

Mrs. Boreslaw Gaj said: "My idea would be to use the phone. I am in agreement with Mr. Richmond. But Mr. Cullen has something on his side too. Why not boycott our telephones one day a week as a further protest?"

The subscribers leaped on this compromise, pleased at being able to line up with both camps. It was decided to leave the receivers off their hooks every Thursday while Farrell remained postmaster. The meeting of the telephone subscribers was adjourned. They filed out of the Town Hall into the frosty night feeling, indeed, as if they had accomplished a great deal.

:8:

EXTRACT from the Official Report, *Parliamentary Debates, Dáil Éireann*, December 13:

Mr Brennan asked the Minister for Posts and Telegraphs if he will state the average weekly turnover in cash and deposits transmitted through Baltinglass Post Office for the past two years.

MR EVERETT: The average weekly turnover at Baltinglass sub-post-office for the past two years was £1130.

Mr Cogan asked the Minister for Posts and Telegraphs whether, in view of the fact that he stated the names of four members of the Dáil and Seanad who recommended Mr Michael Farrell for the position of sub-postmaster in Baltinglass, he will state the names of all other members of the Dáil and Seanad who recommended him.

MR EVERETT: The following members of the Oireachtas * recommended Mr Farrell: Deputies J. Davern, R. Ryan, J. McQuillan, E. Rooney, O. J. Flanagan and Senators A. Fogarty and S. Hayes.

MR COGAN: Is the Minister aware that Deputy Flanagan has claimed that he got the position for Farrell by threatening the Minister that he would expose two Labour scandals and also by getting the Minister for Agriculture, as Deputy Flanagan said, to squeeze the Minister for Posts and Telegraphs, Mr Everett?

MR EVERETT: I wish to deny that emphatically. The Minister for Agriculture never approached me and Deputy Cogan has the wrong facts in connection with this matter as he has them in everything else.

MR COGAN: I have the correct facts.

* The combined Legislatures of Dáil and Senate.

Mr Cogan asked the Minister for Posts and Telegraphs if he will state whether he received a petition signed by the priests and people of Baltinglass strongly recommending Miss H. Cooke for the position of sub-postmistress, the date on which he received it and the nature of his reply to the petition.

MR EVERETT: A memorial signed by the parish priest, a curate and a number of local residents was received in May last in support of Miss H. H. Cooke's application for the position of sub-postmistress of Baltinglass. The memorial was in the form of a recommendation and did not call for a reply.

MR COGAN: Can the Minister state why he defied the priests and the people of Baltinglass and threw an honest, faithful Irish Catholic worker out of employment in defiance——

AN CEANN COMHAIRLE: The Deputy asked for certain information and he has got it.

MR EVERETT: Will the Deputy take the opinion of the people of Baltinglass?

MR COGAN: It has been taken.

Mr Brennan asked the Minister for Posts and Telegraphs if he will state whether the advertisement inviting applications for the position of sub-postmaster in Baltinglass stated that relatives of the retiring sub-postmistress other than immediate blood relatives would not be eligible for appointment; if the advertisement did not contain such an announcement was Miss Cooke held by him to be disqualified for appointment merely on the grounds that she was a relative of the retiring sub-postmistress and if this was not the ground for refusing to appoint her, whether he alleges that the candidate appointed is better qualified than Miss Cooke on (*a*) grounds of general character; (*b*) actual experience of post-office work, or (*c*) steadiness and reliability.

MR EVERETT: The answers to the first and second parts of this question are in the negative. As regards the third part, I would refer the Deputy to my reply to a somewhat similar question by Deputy Cogan on the 6th December.

Mr Brennan asked the Minister for Posts and Telegraphs whether, arising out of the statement made by him in the Dáil Éireann on December 7th that he had appointed Mr M. T. Farrell as sub-postmaster at Baltinglass Post Office because he was the better candidate on the grounds of character, financial stability, etc., it is to be taken that, in the Minister's view: (1) Mr Farrell's character and reputation is better than Miss Cooke's and, if so, whether he will state the grounds for this view; (2) Mr Farrell has more knowledge of the regulations governing the administration of sub-post-offices in towns like Baltinglass; (3) Mr Farrell has had more experience of the management and operation of sub-post-offices and, if this is the Minister's view, whether he will state where Mr Farrell gained such experience; further, whether the Minister's view that Mr Farrell was more generally suitable for the post than Miss Cooke is based on the assumption that Mr Farrell possesses the higher educational qualifications of the two; and, if so, whether the Minister required the candidates to submit themselves to an educational test.

MR EVERETT: I would refer the Deputy to my reply to a somewhat similar question by Deputy Cogan on the 6th December. I have nothing to add to the information given in that reply and in my statement on the 7th December.

MR COGAN: Can the Minister state what recommendation he got from Miss Cooke's immediate superior in Naas? Is it not a fact that the postmaster in Naas emphatically recommended Miss Cooke for this position?

MR BRENNAN: Is the Minister aware of the fact that the people of Baltinglass, who are the best judges of the proper person to fill the position of sub-postmaster in Baltinglass and who have had years of experience—

AN CEANN COMHAIRLE: The Deputy may not make a speech on a supplementary question.

MR BRENNAN: —believe that Miss Cooke should have been appointed and not a henchman of the Minister's?

There was considerable noise in the House at this stage [the *Irish Times* reported], with deputies shouting remarks at each other, and Mr Brennan was heard to refer to "political corruption."

Mr Fahy rang the order bell, however, and insisted on the House passing to the next question.

After the Taoiseach had announced the order of business, Mr M. J. Davern (F.F.) said that in connection with a statement made in the House last Thursday night in which the Minister for Posts and Telegraphs associated him "with the unsavory appointment in Baltinglass" he would like the Chair to allow him to make an explanation, and asked when this would be possible.

THE SPEAKER: Possibly tomorrow.

Mr Brennan asked if the Taoiseach was prepared to indicate whether he intended to allow Government time for the discussion of the motion calling for the setting up of a Select Committee of the House to inquire into all the circumstances surrounding the appointment of a sub-postmaster in Baltinglass.

MR COSTELLO: No: no time for it at all.

Further extract from the Official Report, *Parliamentary Debates, Dáil Éireann*, December 13:

MR COGAN: Can the Taoiseach indicate whether it is the intention of the Government to get up this proposed committee of inquiry?

THE TAOISEACH: It is not.

MR COGAN: Is the Taoiseach aware and—

AN CEANN COMHAIRLE: There is a motion down. No time is being given for it and it cannot be debated now.

MR COGAN: I wonder is the House aware that a picket was instituted against the teacher running the school? Does the House realise that?

AN CEANN COMHAIRLE: The Deputy will resume his seat.

MR COGAN: Is the House aware—

AN CEANN COMHAIRLE: The Deputy will resume his seat.

MR COGAN: —that an attempt was made—

AN CEANN COMHAIRLE: I shall ask the Deputy to leave the House as he refuses to obey the Chair.

MR COGAN: I will leave the House as a protest against the manner in which this matter of Miss Cooke's appointment has been dealt with.

AN CEANN COMHAIRLE: The Deputy will leave the House.

MR COGAN: And as a protest against the attempt to boycott the vocational schoolteacher—

AN CEANN COMHAIRLE: The Deputy will leave the House.

MR COGAN: The only person that can be attacked—

AN CEANN COMHAIRLE: I do not know whether the Deputy desires to be named or not—

Mr Cogan: I call on the House to support this demand for an inquiry.

The Deputy withdrew.

: 9 :

Wednesday (Sheridan said) was a busy day. It dawned foggy and cold, with a thin, fresh fall of snow on the ground. The General arrived at my place shortly after nine o'clock to take me to Dublin.

He says to me: "I'm very much afraid of this weather, Sheridan," he says. "The ceiling is so low for flying. It certainly looks bad."

"But it may not be so bad around Dublin," I say, hoping I am right. We went to Luke McDonald, on the Main Street, and collected the thirty pounds we thought we would need, he having been chosen treasurer of the Protest Committee. Then we headed up the Dublin road in the General's Austin stationwagon. On the way up the General talked about his flying experiences in India, where he had piloted himself around.

"Will you be nervous going up in this weather, Sheridan?" he says after a while.

I thought of poor Miss Cooke being out of a job and counting on us, and I say: "Oh, I'll not be nervous at all." And I kept thinking that maybe the weather would clear up when we got there, and then there would be nothing to be nervous about. By the time we reached Dublin the fog had indeed lifted a little. We drove direct to Ashe's studio at 133 Lower Baggot Street, and the General and I met Ashe face to face for the first time. He was young, younger than I expected, and very tall and thin. I am six feet, and he made me look like a pygmy. He had a bushy brown moustache, and there was something about his face, a look of being able to do things, that gave me confidence in him. The General told Ashe the proposed course—Dublin to Wicklow, Wicklow to Baltinglass, Baltinglass to Carlow, Carlow to Newbridge, Newbridge to Naas, Naas to Dublin.

"How long do you reckon it will take to do that?" he says to Ashe.

"About four hours," Ashe says after he examined the map.

The General was taken aback. "Oh," he says, "we reckoned that your aircraft would do ninety miles per hour, and that it would take about an hour and a half."

Ashe says :"I'm afraid not. Taking into consideration the throttling back of the engine and the time it would take to do each town, four hours is a good estimate."

We both felt crestfallen. We had only thirty pounds to work with, and this would cost us eighty pounds, by simple addition. The General looked at me and lifted his shoulders up in a defeated gesture, and dropped them again. "Well, do your best for us," he says. "Have you had a weather report yet?"

"Yes; but the final information will be picked up at the airport. It doesn't look too good." It was now about half past eleven. I moved over to the window. There was still some fog, and I didn't feel too good about it, but, of course, I made no comment.

Then the General says: "Sheridan, here, will be going with you." There was a choking feeling in my throat. I still said nothing. I was determined to go through with it for Miss Cooke's sake.

"Oh," Ashe says, and paused for a minute. Then he says: "I hadn't reckoned on that. The weight of the equipment and the space it takes, packed in the second seat, makes that impossible. The p-a system and batteries are very heavy, and I'm afraid I have to do the broadcasting myself."

The General turned to me, full of sympathy for my feelings. He cleared his throat. "That's disappointing for you, Sheridan," he says.

"No," I say. "Not at all. I can go to the General Post Office and join in with the picketing. What about this question of finance?" I say, changing the subject.

I turned to Norman Ashe. "We reckoned this would cost thirty pounds, and that's the money we brought." I handed the thirty pounds to him, and he made no word of objection at the amount.

"Well," he says, grinning, "it's unusual for me to be paid in advance. Generally I have to wait for my payment." He took the money and made out a receipt. "I'm glad," he says, "to fly and to broadcast for such a cause." I felt very relieved. We parted company then—Ashe for the airport, General Dennis to attend to private business, and me for the G.P.O.

When I got there I saw a battery of press photographers waiting on the steps. They saw me at the same time. For a minute all I could see was the white splashes of flash bulbs going off. A reporter says to me: "What time are the pickets coming from Baltinglass?" Another says: "Where are they?"

I waited until the stars from the flash bulbs faded from my eyes. "How do you people know we're putting a picket on the G.P.O.?" I say. They didn't tell me.

The picketers arrived at two o'clock, a little later than planned, as Paddy O'Grady had had some difficulty in getting all the posters finished by Coventry. They, too, were greeted by a barrage of flash bulbs. A crowd began to gather.

"Good for Baltinglass!" they yelled. "That's the stuff to give them!"

Passing motorists held up their thumbs. While three or four photographers were asking us to stop and pose for a picture a policeman came over. "I'm sorry," he says, "but you'll have to keep on the move." The picket marched up O'Connell Street and around the Parnell monument.

"There was a man," I say in a loud voice, "who was against the like of what the Government did to Miss Cooke." And a man in the crowd following us says: "Yes! Keep it up, Baltinglass!"

We kept marching up and down the length of O'Connell Street, with Kitty Patterson and Lucy Doyle distributing handbills as we went.

The day passed off without incident. The Gardai and the people smiled when we passed. No one seemed to disapprove of what we were doing. Afterwards we went to a hotel and had a mixed grill for supper, and all of us went to see an Abbott and Costello film before we went back home to Baltinglass.

: 10 :

NORMAN ASHE wallowed round in the air over Dublin and its suburbs. For better audibility he had had a silencer installed on his small Auster aircraft.

Below, on the pavement of Mount Merrion Avenue, in Black Rock, a Mr. Muldoon and a Mr. Fogarty were passing the time of the day.

"What the hell's that?" Fogarty said suddenly. "I thought I heard some one saying: 'Baltinglass calling'!"

"Me, too," Muldoon replied, looking round and frowning. The two men looked up and down the street. They looked every way but straight up.

"Damned if I know what it was," Fogarty said, shaking his head slowly. "I could have sworn I heard it, but I'm damned if I can *see* anything."

And in Cabra, Inchicore, Drimnagh, Kimmage, Dundrum, Stillorgan, Lun Laoghaire, and Bray others heard Norman Ashe's voice coming to them out of the sky through the twin loudspeakers on the wings of his Auster.

"Baltinglass calling . . . Baltinglass calling . . . Baltinglass demands clean administration. The people of Baltinglass need your support. Our fight is your fight."

: 11 :

On Wednesday, December 13, Mr. T. Roycroft, General Secretary of the Clann na Poblachta, one of the parties in Mr. Costello's coalition, received a letter from the Baltinglass branch of the party.

Dear Mr Roycroft,

The Party, during the election campaign, made it known that it would not stand for anything but clean Government: you now stand by and allow a grave injustice to be done on two defenceless women. The appointment of Michael Farrell as postmaster of Baltinglass is one of the many glaring cases of political jobbery that are being enacted during the inter-party Government's term of office.

You are a party to it and, therefore, must accept the responsibility for their actions. I suppose the Ministers will be doing their best to qualify for their pensions on February 28, but if the Clann had any respect for themselves and their followers, they would not stand for [this appointment] for the sake of their pensions.

Miss Katie Cooke, who is now eighty-two years of age, and who has been an invalid in the last six months, gets no pension after a lifetime of public service. What does she get? Firstly, a death sentence, because the little comforts, the medical attention and the necessities of life were provided by the money her niece earned for her as postmistress. Secondly, she got what amounted to an eviction, as you will see by Press reports and photographs. As one person commented: "The days of the Land League are back."

I now wish to state that the local branch of the Clann na Poblachta is dissolved, and, therefore, we do not want any further communication or contacts directed to us.

The letter was signed by Patrick O'Grady, the Baltinglass Branch Secretary of the Clann na Poblachta, on behalf of the branch's committee.

: 12 :

EXTRACT from the Official Report, *Parliamentary Debates, Dáil Éireann*, December 14:

PERSONAL EXPLANATIONS BY DEPUTIES

MR DAVERN: The Minister for Posts and Telegraphs yesterday, in giving his explanation for his selection of a sub-postmaster in Baltinglass, brought in my name. I wish to state that my recommendation was made in response to a request by an F.C.A. officer who asked me for it on the grounds that an F.C.A. officer was an applicant for the position. As I thought it right that membership of the F.C.A. should be taken into account in making these appointments, I gave a recommendation some seven or eight months ago. I did not know Mr Farrell. Neither did I know the local circumstances. I had no idea that his appointment, would be the cause of depriving a lady, who had fourteen years' faithful service behind her, of her position. The recommendation of the other member of my Party—

AN CEANN COMHAIRLE: The Deputy is speaking for himself in a personal explanation and a personal explanation cannot include anyone but himself.

MR DAVERN: In any case I find it hard to believe that a recommendation from me or other members of the Fianna Fáil Party—

An Ceann Comhairle: That has nothing to do with a personal explanation.

Mr Davern: —was the determining consideration with the Minister responsible for the making of this selection.

An Ceann Comhairle: The Deputy has exceeded his promise to me.

Minister for Posts and Telegraphs (Mr Everett): I can appreciate the Deputy's embarrassment and the embarrassment of his Party.

Mr Lemass: What is happening now?

An Ceann Comhairle: There is no debate on the matter.

Mr Everett: "No better man—"

Mr Lemass: Go away and hide your head in shame.

Mr Everett: "No better man could be found for the job," he said.

An Ceann Comhairle: Deputy Flanagan.

Mr Flanagan: I shall be extremely brief. Unfortunately I was unavoidably absent from the House yesterday due to the fact that I had to attend a meeting of the estimates committee of the local—

An Ceann Comhairle: That has nothing to do with it.

Mr Flanagan: I noticed in the morning papers,

and I heard it on the radio last night, that my name was mentioned in the House yesterday by a Deputy in connection with the appointment of a postmaster at Baltinglass. A Deputy asked the Minster for Posts and Telegraphs for the names of those who recommended a particular applicant.

AN CEANN COMHAIRLE: Would the Deputy briefly state how he is affected in the matter?

MR FLANAGAN: My name was amongst the names of those Deputies who, the Minister said, recommended Mr Farrell. I certainly recommended Mr Farrell. I was given to understand that the applicant had no job and that he had been working on his grandfather's farm until it was sold twelve months ago. I certainly made very strong representations to the Minister.

AN CEANN COMHAIRLE: The Deputy rose on a particular point which he promised me he would raise; he has not done so yet.

MR FLANAGAN: I understand that Deputy Cogan made a statement in the House to the effect that I used threats to induce the Minister for Posts and Telegraphs to make this appointment. I assure both the Chair and the House that that statement is quite untrue. I made no threats. I recommended Mr Farrell. I stand over my recommendation. I would do the same again if the opportunity occurred. If this Government cannot stand over and defend its appointments, then it should take up the challenge issued by the Leader of the Opposition, Deputy de Valera, and go to the people on a general election.

Interruptions.

AN CEANN COMHAIRLE: Order.

MR FLANAGAN: If we make an appointment we shall stand over it and I stand over my recommendation in this case.

AN CEANN COMHAIRLE: I will not have any more of that.

MR T. BRENNAN: I would like to make an explanation.

AN CEANN COMHAIRLE: The Deputy asked me if he might rise on a matter in which he thought he was aggrieved. I read over the debate and I do not see anything in it to which the Deputy should object. In the second place, the Deputy was present when the statement to which he now objects was made. The rule is that if a statement is made in the House to which a Deputy objects, because he thinks it reflects upon him, he must make his objection at the time the statement is made. We cannot have points of explanation days afterwards from people who were present at the time the statement was made. I do not think that either the Deputy's honour or integrity was impugned in the slightest degree by the statement to which he now wishes to refer.

MR T. BRENNAN: Do you mean to suggest that

where a deliberate statement that I supported an appeal to the young men of the country to join the L.D.F.—

An Ceann Comhairle: I might say, though perhaps it is not my function to do so, that members of the L.D.F. were promised they would be considered for office later and might get some preference. I do not think there is anything wrong in that.

Mr T. Brennan: I never made such a statement. It is grossly inaccurate and it is quite untrue. It is most unfair on the part of the Minister for Posts and Telegraphs to make the reference he did.

The Taoiseach: It is proposed that the House on its adjournment today will adjourn until 14th February, 1951.

: 13 :

And, during the cold, grey dawn of Wednesday, as if enough had not already gone on in the Dáil to call indignant attention to the Baltinglass battle, another group of unknown Cooke sympathizers—or, indeed, could it have been the same stubborn band as did a similar job before?—sawed through some more telephone poles and snipped through some more telephone wires. In fact, when the post-office linesmen finally located the breaks, they found that while within a few miles of Baltinglass itself seven poles were sawn off at about a foot above snow level there was still another piece of the same kind of sabotage far to the north and twenty-five long miles away.

Of course, this was not a matter to be taken lightly by the Gardai, and it was not long before patrols of blue-uniformed men, looking grim and purposeful in their sleek, shining cars, travelled about the countryside, full of questions and queries, full of sharp suspicious searchings for clues, pressed from behind for results as they were by their superior officers, but not getting any. It was amazing how so many poles had been sawn and so many wires snipped in the deathly silence of the winter night, when the snapping sound of a twig would have startled a rabbit three fields away; it was amazing that no one had heard the men who did it, and that no passer-by had seen them as they pulled and pushed, pulled and pushed at their cross-cut saws in the ghostly gloom. Yet, surely, the amateur detectives were saying to one another that day in public houses from Kilcullen to Colbinstown, surely there would be the footprints, the tire-tracks? Surely there would be clues a-plenty for the bluecoats to sift so that they could put their fingers on the culprits? But no: there were no arrests that day. And someone, at a meeting of the Protest Committee in Baltinglass, even suggested that the job might have been done by the Little People, since it was obvious and clear whose side *they* would be on if the fight reached into another dimension.

Still, the linesmen had their own problems to deal with, and they went to work with a will; by one o'clock in that same afternoon the repairs to the line were completed and communications between Baltinglass and Dublin were, as people in official places are inclined to put it, "restored to normal." They had just begun to breathe easily in Dublin headquarters about this when, at eleven o'clock that night, the blow fell. "Baltinglass is isolated," an unhappy telephone-worker informed his chief, who was at home, preparing for bed, but quickly changed his mind and his direction. Yes, the wires had been cut again.

By this time even Mr. Costello and his friends were beginning to realize that the use of a large, uniformed force against the Cooke army had, from a public-relations viewpoint, been a mistake. Because of it the Battle of Baltinglass had not—as expected—been damped out; instead it had burst its bounds. Loyal Cooke supporters had won new recruits here and there, north and south, east and west, in town and country, and even beyond the seas. Somehow, where the experienced and canny Government forces had gone wrong, the pick-up Protest Committee in little Baltinglass, with no prior exercise in such matters, had stumbled on exactly the right formula to attract the attention of, and the sympathy of, the common people of Ireland. When the press was needed they

saw to it that there was a story the press would want
to use, instinctively reaching out for the basic plank
in the science of publicity. And—another basic—
they did not let a good story die, so that the press
would not let it die. Pickets, protests, public-address
systems, aeroplanes, politics, private post-office, and
Christian pleas for peace—nothing was allowed to
escape the attention of the press, and, through the
press, the people up and down the land. Until now,
at last, an appetite had been created among the people to read, and among the press to print, anything,
trivial or not, having to do with the Baltinglass affair.

To combat this advantage there were those on the
other side—although not by any means all—who
were ready to use whatever ammunition they could
find. One Farrell supporter, who would now prefer
to be nameless, and who shall be, tried to bring the
question of religion into his argument against Miss
Cooke, saying as he did that she had been born in
Scotland and of non-Catholic parents, and insinuating
that, in a country largely composed of Irish Catholics, one who was neither had no right to hold public
office. Another Cooke opponent suggested that she
did not have Michael Farrell's educational qualifications. A third indicated his strong opinion that, since
young Farrell was unemployed and Miss Cooke was
not, he should have her job; a piece of reasoning not
without its self-contained entanglement.

It was on Thursday, December 14, that Helen

Cooke sat down and wrote to the press a long letter in her own defence, a letter to be read by thousands, discussed and argued, praised by many, and blamed by some.

"I have waited some considerable time," Helen Cooke wrote,

hoping that there might be found one man in the Cabinet who was willing to forgo place and pension in order that he might defend justice. My character has been taken away where I was unable to defend it. This does not worry me, but I never thought that Holy Ireland would fall so low. I have, therefore, to ask you to kindly print the following:

At the closing date for application Mr Michael Farrell had two nominations. I had a form signed by ninety per cent. of the shopkeepers, headed by Very Rev. Patrick Doyle, P.P., V.G., and the curate, and seven letters from prominent citizens, State Solicitors, Bank Managers, etc. When townspeople examined the two application forms in Dublin a couple of weeks ago, my application had only one recommendation attached. Mr Farrell's two recommendations were increased to numerous ones, including T.D.'s. Who inserted these after the closing date? The townspeople were also informed that the appointment was made three weeks previously. Head Office was informed the day before I was, namely the 23rd November, 1950. Why did it take three weeks for the letter to go to Naas?

My father was born and bred in Baltinglass. I was born in Scotland and my mother was Scotch. My parents on both sides were born Catholics, and so am I by the Grace of God. My grandfather, John Brown, Dunclutha, Greenock, housed Parnell, whilst on a visit to Scotland. I purposely did not bring religion into this matter previously, as even if I were a non-Catholic I am still entitled to justice.

Premises: Our premises have been noted as being one of the best under Naas. Farrell's are smaller and adjoin their public house. Rule 17, pages 15 to 18, Rules for Sub-Postmasters, states:

Connection with, ownership or management of public house, forbidden. (*a*) Officers of the Department are forbidden to be connected with, directly or indirectly, the ownership or management of an inn or public house, or any establishment licensed for the sale of drink to be consumed on the premises. (*b*) While it may sometimes be necessary to appoint as sub-postmaster a person holding a licence for the sale of drink to be consumed off the premises, no person already in the service of the Department can be permitted to take any steps to acquire such a licence without the previous sanction of the Minister for Posts and Telegraphs, and the owner of an existing licence, without such permission, must not apply for any other form of licence for the sale of drink. (*c*) Such sanction, if given, will be subject in all cases to the condition that no liquor is sold except in closed vessels.

Financial position: Whilst we are not in debt, we have no means, neither can I support my aunt in Baltinglass. Mr Farrell has no dependents, and the family have a public house, grocery, drapery, butcher's stall, and land.

Education: Did Mr Farrell pass an examination at College? I went to school in Galway, Dominican Convent, Taylor's Hill, and to St Mary of the Isle, Cork. I passed senior grade in Cork, taking Honours in two subjects and passing in Honours in a third. When I lived in Healthfield Road, Dublin, during Free State rule, I was associated with underground Press movement in Cadogan Road. I am known to be an Irish Republican all my life, and am an Irish citizen by my father's nationality and by preference. I have fourteen years of experience and of complete charge in post-office.

The accounts show a daily turnover fluctuating from £600 to £3000 a day, not a year.

An official from Head Office (Naas) was sent

to interview applicants, to examine premises and investigate character for position when advertised. Why is this report kept secret? I have never spoken to the Minister for Posts and Telegraphs in my life. He has never been on our premises during the past fourteen years, if ever before then.

Underground cable: Before this was installed the officials stated that I had to assure them that I would never resign from the Post Office, as otherwise it would entail a colossal expense on the Department. Wages were paid to linesmen, etc., of approximately £50 per week over a period of three months. This did not include numerous visits by higher ranking officials, and their cars, or the cost of the cable and other material.

I do not think it should be beyond even a junior counsel to see the want of logic in removing an existing cable in case I might retire or be too old in ten years' time. The age limit is sixty for this appointment. My aunt was appointed at the age of sixty-eight years.

The Minister for Posts and Telegraphs states that I was not an employee of the Department. A Regulation was made lately and approved by the Department that in cases of vacancies an employee of the Department would obtain preference. Rule 20 (b), pages 19 to 21, Rules for Sub-postmasters, reads:

According to the definition in Section 89 of the Post Office Act, 1908, the expression "Officer of the Post Office" includes any person employed in any business of the Department, whether employed by the Minister for Posts and Telegraphs, or by any person under him or on behalf of the Department.

Cheques for hundreds of pounds have been made out in my name over a period of years, and solely in my name for the past eight months.

I regret trespassing on your valuable space, but in the interests of fair play to the humblest of the land I believe you will do a great service to Ireland in making the above known. Whether this is replied to by the Government or allowed to go unheeded as in the Dáil, I am certain that the public will be able to judge who is speaking the truth.

Thursday, December 14, was the day the supporters of Helen Cooke boycotted their telephones. A slight thaw had set in, making the roads dangerously slippery for automobile traffic. Nevertheless, when Sheridan found it necessary to put through a call to Dublin, he drove to Castledermot, several miles away, and phoned from there. That night a Protest Committee meeting was held at Felix O'Neill's.

General Meade Dennis, seated before the fire in his library at Fortgranite House, thought about his two tenants, the Farrells and the Cookes, on opposite

sides of the Battle of Baltinglass. He was sorry that
the Farrells had not accepted his well-intended invi-
tation to drop out of the battle, because he knew he
could not let the matter rest as it was, and he re-
gretted the action he was about to take, and the need
to take it. Yet he could see no other way. Presently,
like Helen Cooke, he too composed a letter, guiding
his pen precisely over his carefully chosen words.

DEAR MR COSTELLO,

As you have consistently refused to see me or to
receive a deputation from Baltinglass on the question of the appointment by your Minister for Posts
and Telegraphs of Mr Michael Farrell to the
position of Sub-Postmaster, I feel it my duty to
write to you.

The merits of Miss Cooke's qualifications must
by now be well known to you, as well as the
strength of feeling in the country on the question,
and I do not intend to go into them in this letter.
But you may have formed the impression that I
have some personal antagonism to Mr Farrell and
his family. This is far from being the case. Mr
Everett, being a close personal friend of the family, must be well aware that not long ago, I, as
Mrs Farrell's landlord, was in a position to give
her considerable help in the matter of her lease,
and that I willingly gave that help to a family
whom I have known since childhood, and with

whom neither my father nor I have ever been on other than friendly terms. My personal feelings have only been aroused by the grave wrong that I see being done to Miss Katie Cooke in her old age, and to her niece who has served the State honourably and without fault for many years. From your only public statement, it would appear that you have set your face against any form of public inquiry, and have accepted the statements of the Minister for Posts and Telegraphs, some of which do, in fact, require corroboration.

Mr Everett has stated in the Dáil, in answer to a question, that "not the majority" of the people of Baltinglass are fighting for the rights of Miss Cooke. If he is sincere in this belief, he has been badly misinformed, and I suggest that he should take a referendum of the postal area served by the Baltinglass Post Office. Mention has been made on his behalf, if not by him, of suitability of premises. The old post-office has been most suitable for over seventy years. The new one is installed in a licensed premises. The whole of this premises is covered by the licence, and, as landlord, I believe I am entitled to object to any restriction of the licence which must, of necessity, reduce the value of my property.

He has also stated that the appointment was made on grounds of character and financial stability. Comparisons of this nature are objectionable, and it would be neither right nor proper for me to discuss them.

You may feel that to have given way to the protest made in Baltinglass would have been a submission to mob law, and would have created an unfortunate precedent. We are only too well aware from the history of this country that mob law results inevitably from misrule. Our democratic machinery gives us the right to elect our own government to rule over our affairs; if it fails in that task, or if misrule creeps in, the people must speak out.

The question of the appointment of the subpostmaster in a small village would be a matter of little consequence in these tremendous days in which we live, were it not that it has brought up the whole principle of clean administration, and hits right at the roots of democratic government.

The General posted copies of his letter to the Dublin morning papers, as well as to the Prime Minister. Later he called round to see Mrs. Farrell, accompanied by his solicitor. ("I went to her," he explained afterwards, "solely and simply to protect my lease from infringements.")

The lawyer spoke first. "You have broken the lease, Mrs. Farrell, by making structural alterations. You realize that you could legally be ejected?"

"Now, Mrs. Farrell," Dennis broke in hurriedly, anxious that there be no misunderstanding, "I want you to understand that I will never eject you. I've known you too long. But I cannot allow any part of these premises to be delicensed, thereby devaluing the worth of the premises."

Mrs. Farrell looked at the General coldly. She looked at his solicitor coldly. "Good afternoon, gentlemen," said Mrs. Farrell, a large and determined woman. "Good afternoon to you." But it was observed that she seemed to be considering and debating with herself when they left. Even now it is difficult to assess the place this move of the General's had in the final result of the Battle of Baltinglass, but there is little enough doubt that it caused the Farrells to think. For if the law said that the sub-post-office could not be maintained on a licensed premises, and they had no premises which could be delicensed, where would the post-office be?

Extract from the "letters to the editor" column of the *Irish Times:*

THE BALTINGLASS POST

Sir, In view of the general disquiet caused by the recent Baltinglass appointment, it is only just that Miss Cooke's letter in your issue of this date should receive a reply from the Minister for Posts and Telegraphs.

An objective perusal of Miss Cooke's communication regarding her qualifications *vis-à-vis* the Minister's statement in the Dáil, tends to augment further the general diffidence in the Minister's decision.

In defence of his selection of the successful candidate, the Minister relied on the facts that his appointee had a college education, his character, financial stability, etc., were good, he was thirty years younger [than his rival] he had served in the L.D.F., and is now a member of the F.C.A.

Miss Cooke has not only a college [convent] education, but in the Senior Grade examination took honours in two subjects and passed with honours in a third—no mean achievement. Her character or financial stability was not challenged by the Minister. She gave her services to the Irish Republican cause. Loyal to her national principles, she was associated with the underground Press movement (anyone who has experience of the perils of this undertaking can estimate the sacrifice demanded). She has had fourteen years' experience of complete charge of a post-office. According to the Minister, she would be able to perform her duties for another ten years or so.

Faced with these data, it is difficult to reconcile with reason the Minister's statement in the Dáil on December 7th, 1950:

The strongest point, however, in Miss Cooke's favour, so far as I can judge from the arguments put forward, was that members of her family had held the office over a long period of years.

Many readers will conclude that the strongest point in Miss Cooke's favour is contained in her letter to the Press. To that letter an official reply is imperative. Otherwise, the Minister and the Government must take the consequences.

The disemployment of this lady without just cause, and her enforced emigration to make a living for herself and her enfeebled aunt, are matters which test seriously the claim of this State to be termed Christian.

During the past week the Government were asked to allot time for the discussion of a simple motion, which, if not acceptable to them in the terms of its construction, could have been amended to secure that the essentials of the proposal would have been clarified.

Heretofore, communications between deputies and senators with each other and with Ministers, normally have been regarded as confidential. It is regrettable that representations made by members of the Oireachtas should have been publicised, and, in this regard, it is still more distressing that, in the first instance, only names of the opposition were mentioned in relation to the Baltinglass vacancy.

Yours, etc.,

J. P. BRENNAN, T.D.

DÁIL ÉIREANN (LEINSTER HOUSE), DUBLIN
December 16th, 1950

Well, what with letters to the press and letters to the Prime Minister and the people being aroused, and what with never knowing when or where the telephone lines would be cut next—or what, indeed, was likely to happen, and without warning—the men in high places were feeling the ends of their nerves and wondering and waiting. And who could blame them? Who could blame them, for instance, if they were all the more determined to catch the ones who cut down the poles and snipped the wires in the dark of night? Who could blame them for putting teams of Gardai on all-day and all-night patrol along the highways, and for putting their own secret service on the job—namely, three plain-clothes detectives—to do what they could in the way of counterintelligence?

: 14 :

To look at Miss Trasa MacGeehan no one would have suspected that she might become involved in the flamboyant action of the Battle of Baltinglass. A mouse-haired spinster in her forties, she was tall, angular, ailing, and run down. She lived in Harcourt Terrace, deep in the heart of Dublin town; and she was a personal friend of long standing of Deputy Cogan, none other. The fact is that in a roundabout way it was through him that she became involved in the case. It was Cogan, months before, who had first made her aware of the suspenseful situation Miss Cooke found herself in; and then, when Michael Farrell was given the job of sub-postmaster, he told her about that, too, commenting on the injustice of it.

Trasa MacGeehan had clucked her tongue with proper sympathy. "I know of at least a dozen similar cases," she had told Paddy Cogan, thinking to comfort him, but not succeeding. Then she said, musing, and not believing there was really any contribution she could make, ailing as she was: "I wonder if there is any way I could help?"

"Would you really be wanting to, Trasa? Would you be well enough?"

"Perhaps if I could do something which would not require too much time and effort—something that wouldn't tax too heavily on my strength . . ."

"Yes," Cogan said, nodding thoughtfully. "Well, we'll see. We'll see." And for a while Trasa Mac-Geehan thought no more about it, although she was eager and anxious to help Miss Cooke. Indeed, she had not yet met the lady, but, measuring her by

Paddy Cogan's description, she already considered her to be the finest type of Irishwoman. What was the use of wanting to help, she thought, sighing, when she was lacking the health to do it?

That Friday scattered shots were exchanged across the battlefront. About eighty Farrell supporters, still basking in the glow of their Government-reinforced victory, assembled that evening carrying fifteen lighted peat-torches, and marched up the Main Street and into the Town Hall. It had been rumoured, to the astonishment of the Cooke forces, that Mr. Everett was coming into Baltinglass, straight into their stronghold, to address the Farrell meeting. To show how *they* felt about the Minister, merchants—normally open for business—who favoured the white-haired Helen shut their shops and pulled their blinds. Christmas might be only a few days away, and every opening hour a boon to their tills, but this, they felt, was too much to take unprotesting. Meanwhile Deputy Cogan dropped into a Protest Committee meeting, where he was made welcome.

"I was talking to Trasa MacGeehan, a friend of mine, in Dublin yesterday," Cogan said, sounding them out. "She's anxious to form a protest sub-committee there if she has your approval."

"Sure, and she has it," Ben Hooper said without hesitation. "That's what we want: we want committees everywhere." The other committee men agreed, and Bernie Sheridan was delegated to telephone Miss MacGeehan next day.

He did so. "That is a magnificent idea of yours," Sheridan told her. "The one, I mean, about forming a Dublin Protest Committee."

Pleased with his enthusiasm, Trasa MacGeehan warmed to the subject. "Oh, Mr. Sheridan," she said, "I thought perhaps I could collect signatures of protest." She calculated that this work would make few demands on her time and on her strength, neither of which she had in abundance.

"Sure, and go ahead with it," Sheridan said. "We're all behind you in Baltinglass."

She wrote at once to the Dublin papers, appealing to Irish men and women for moral support and for ten thousand signatures of protest against the way the Government had treated Helen Cooke. Before Miss MacGeehan arose from her bed, on the day her letter was published, nine signatures were handed in the door to her housekeeper. The evening post brought another eighteen. From then on they came in an unending, multiplying flood, and it was not long before her goal was reached and passed.

There began, too, a continuous stream of cars, bringing lists of signatures to her door from all the counties of Ireland—both North and South. Letters containing signatures and protests soon came from places as far distant as Australia, South Africa, England, Scotland, Wales, Canada, and the United States of America. One girl, an employee of the Irish Sweepstakes office in Ballbridge, doggedly collected four hundred signatures, and shyly brought them in with the query: "Would you like to have some more now?"

And thus it was that the job meant to spare her health kept Trasa MacGeehan busy from early morning until late night—answering queries, accepting signatures, and refusing, with gentle insistence, offers of cash for the cause. A rest, indeed! And yet, at that time, she had still not met Helen Cooke.

: 15 :

THERE was a lull in the battle on Saturday, with little reconnoitring on either side, and, in fact, the Cooke supporters were giving the Farrell store a wide berth both with their persons and their patronage. But on Sunday, beginning with Father Doyle's proxy appeal—by letter—from all Masses in the parish, things began to hum again.

"We are very sorry to learn," said the letter from the Very Reverend gentleman,

that there has been cutting of telegraph poles recently in the Baltinglass district and outside it. This destruction of public property is morally wrong and might result in serious punishment for any persons caught and brought to justice. We beseech all sections of the community to set their faces firmly against a repetition of the acts here or elsewhere.

And there it was. With the priest ill in his bed with heart trouble, and the people properly respectful of him at any rate, there wasn't much chance that the sabotage would be repeated if anyone from Baltinglass had anything to do with it. Of course, none from the village *had* been involved in the cutting of the poles or the snipping of the wires: this was understood. Still, the letter from Father Doyle reached out a long way—even, apparently, to such places as Kilcullen and Colbinstown, and there were no more acts of sabotage even there.

It was not, however, the priest's letter that set most of the tongues to wagging on Sunday, but the arrival from Cork of Owen O'Mahony, barrister and Knight of Malta. Indeed, while Owen O'Mahony was the name in his family Bible, he was far better known throughout the hills and plains of Ireland as "The Pope." Why he was called this nobody seemed to know, unless it was that in certain quarters he was thought to be a saintly man and a champion of the downtrodden. He was reputed, also, to have influence in political circles, although how the saintliness and the politics were able to walk hand in hand nobody took the trouble to consider.

Yet it was none of those things that opened the eyes and loosened the tongues of the good people of Baltinglass. Small townsfolk in every land are apt to stare hardest at what they are not used to and what they do not expect. Thus, when Owen O'Mahony rode up in his Austin station-wagon and then climbed out of it onto the pavement of the Main Street in his short, white, flannel coat, his black trousers, his heavy black boots—shined so well the toecaps were like twin mirrors—with no hat on and no overcoat, although it was freezing cold and the snow was knit tight to the ground, the ones who saw him first stared and then gasped and finally turned to one another incredulously and exchanged their honest views. They exchanged views on his beard, turning white already, although he could not, they agreed, be more than forty-five or, perhaps, -six. They exchanged views on his round face and fair complexion, and on how it was that, in spite of the eccentricity of his dress, he left the impression of culture and breeding. And, mostly, they exchanged views and speculations as to why he had come to Baltinglass at all.

And why *would* a man like Owen O'Mahony come to a place like Baltinglass in the dead of winter, with no fishing to be had in the frigid Slaney, with the inns full of people from the press, with Christmas close at hand? Why, indeed! If he were a champion of the downtrodden, where could he find anyone more downtrodden—and with the Protest Committee and the press of the world to publicize her position—than Miss Helen Cooke? And that was the answer, of course: "The Pope" was here to investigate for himself the rights and wrongs of the case, and to offer his help if it were needed. He hadn't seen anyone in the town then, and he didn't quite know where to start until he saw a poster—BALTINGLASS DEMANDS JUSTICE: EVERETT MUST GO—in the window of Patrick O'Grady's house. He knocked at the door, and Mrs. O'Grady presented herself. From there on he moved round Baltinglass quickly, talking to every one he could meet who was in any way—and on either side —connected with the affair. He called on The O'Mahony, at Grangecon, and on Major-General Dennis at draughty Fortgranite House, and on Ben Hooper, the headmaster of the Technical School, and on Father Doyle, in his sick-bed. It had been suggested to him in certain Farrell circles that it was not Father Doyle himself who had written the letter signed by his name and sent to Mr. Costello, the Prime Minister. Owen O'Mahony asked the priest straight out if he had written it.

"I dictated it to Ben Hooper and signed it myself," Father Doyle said. And "The Pope" was satisfied.

It was Paddy O'Grady whom Owen O'Mahony sent to bring Bernie Sheridan to him, after he had gone round and seen the people and made up his mind regarding the rights and wrongs of the case. Sheridan had been busy with other matters concerning the battle, and had not heard much of Mr. O'Mahony's stay in Baltinglass, except a remark or two passed by Maureen when he wasn't entirely listening.

"Come on, Bernie," O'Grady said to him, " 'The Pope' would like to see you."

"Who?" Sheridan asked, looking at O'Grady in a peculiar, disbelieving way.

" 'The Pope!' " O'Grady repeated impatiently. "You know, Owen O'Mahony, the gentleman from Cork."

"Oh," Sheridan said, relieved, and followed his friend out of the door into the Main Street. They walked along together, with Sheridan lagging and O'Grady trying to get him to move along with more enthusiasm and speed.

Sheridan stopped in the middle of the pavement.

"Do you *know* this man, Paddy?"

O'Grady shook his head. "Not other than that he's a barrister," he said, "and that he's from Cork. Come along!"

"I see," Sheridan said, hanging back. "You know, we want to be very careful in what we say to strangers."

"All right , you be careful," O'Grady said. They walked on. "And here we are."

Sheridan met "The Pope," and they shook hands. ("It was a bit of a shock, I admit," he said later, "but a man has the right to dress as he likes in a democracy.")

Owen O'Mahony spoke warmly to Sheridan, warmly and approvingly. "I've followed the Baltinglass affair in the public press," he said. "It's a great day for democracy."

"Yes, it is," Sheridan admitted warily.

"I've met some of the people around the town," the man from Cork continued; "Father Moran and Mr. Hooper and General Dennis and Father Doyle and some of the others. And I've met Miss Helen Cooke, a fine, courageous woman. I've talked to dozens of the people of the town, I would say, on both sides of the controversy."

"Indeed," Sheridan said.

"You people are putting up a grand fight," "The Pope" said then, "but Miss Cooke has no chance to win her case. The forces stacked against her are too powerful. I now make her the offer of a constituency in Cork, and I, myself, will support her candidature for the Dáil in the next election. Being a victimized person, she would have a popular appeal to the electors."

"It's a grand offer," Sheridan admitted, warming to the man. He thought: "Maybe he's right: there's always a chance that we would not win our fight for Miss Cooke." Then he said: "It's a question that you will have to put to Miss Cooke in person."

"That would be best," Owen O'Mahony said. They walked down to Miss Cooke's together, and the newcomer placed his offer before her.

Miss Cooke smiled gratefully at him.

"Indeed, thank you very much," she said, without undue excitement. "I will consider the matter, although I would rather be sub-postmistress of Baltinglass."

: 16 :

INDEED, and the visit of Owen O'Mahony touched off some sparks, although most of them did not seem to find tinder until a considerable while later. For instance, there was the newspaper story that came of it, which appeared in the *Irish Times* on December 20.

MISS COOKE MAY BE SENT TO DÁIL

It was learned last night that Miss Cooke, the former Baltinglass sub-postmistress, had been asked to stand as an independent candidate for a Cork constituency in the next general election. A prominent Corkman has offered to support her candidature. She told an *Irish Times* reporter last night that she would give the matter consideration.

Miss Cooke has spent the last few days replying to hundreds of letters which she received from many parts of the country, and from Britain. Among the letters from Britain were some from

Irish exiles asking her to go to England, where she would "get justice."

One of the letters from England related a case where a sub-post-office was closed, when a general post-office was opened, and although the sub-post-mistress was fifty years of age, she got pensionable employment in the new office, at the maximum rate of wages.

Another development yesterday was the resignation from the Fine Gael party, because of the transfer of the sub-post-office, of Mr Felix O'Neill, secretary of the West Wicklow Fine Gael Executive. Mr O'Neill is a member of the Protest Committee and has been associated with the Fine Gael party all his life. He has been secretary since last year.

Two of the three assistants whom Miss Cooke employed have secured other employment: Miss Bridie Scully, Rathvilly, and Miss Marcus Gavin in Baltinglass. The third girl, Miss Marie Farrell, has remained with Miss Cooke.

Letters and parcels are still leaving the town by private cars and postage vans from elsewhere.

: 17 :

AT one stage in his campaign Mick Farrell, a handsome young man with a thick neck and an unexpect-

edly thin voice, had come right out on a public platform and claimed the support of "the farmers and
of the plain Irish people of Baltinglass." Now that,
by itself, was a statement which caused the sensitive
hackles to rise on the napes of the gentlemen of the
Protest Committee, and when Farrell blandly added
that those who sided with him numbered more than
half the total population of the postal district they
let out a mighty, roaring chorus of protest. They
roared again, in even greater pain, when Mr. Everett, the Minister for Posts and Telegraphs, expressed
doubts, in the privileged air of the Dáil, that the
majority of the citizens of Baltinglass supported
Miss Cooke. For this indeed cut them to the quick
of their own argument, and this they could not ignore.

Without wasting any more time in discussing it
than necessary, they promptly decided to settle the
burning question of which side had the majority support in Baltinglass on the subject of the battle for the
sub-postmastership. They decided to do it by holding
a referendum of all those on the voters' register in
the area concerned.

Soon the village and the district seethed with
activity as teams of Cooke supporters curry-combed
the area for signatures of all those in favour of Miss
Cooke. When they were done they claimed 87 per
cent of the registered voters in the postal district to
have cast their votes in favour of the Protest Committee and Miss Cooke.

Yes, blow was being struck for every blow. Indeed, the tempo had speeded up to a pitch that had even the newspapers dizzy—with at least one front-page story every day, sometimes two or three—and now, at last, the sheer weight of the varied and never-ceasing activities of the Protest Committee had its first stunning effect upon the opposition.

In the Dáil the two sides of the House were closely, even skittishly balanced, with the Government having an anxious coalition majority of a mere fourteen seats, including a toll of five political parties and a group of thirteen independents, over the solid and unbroken opposition of the Fianna Fáil Party led by Mr. Eamon de Valera. For a while the coalition had held the balance of power, thinly and precariously, but all at once the dam seemed to break. The leaks had come earlier, of course; first when Deputy Cogan declared that he could not support the Government in the Dáil so long as the injustice to Miss Cooke existed, then when the Baltinglass branch of the Clann na Poblachta dissolved itself and when Felix O'Neill had resigned as secretary to the West Wicklow branch of the Fine Gael Party, and, later, when the Westmeath County Convention of the Clann na Poblachta called for the resignation of Mr. Everett unless the Baltinglass affair was straightened out to the satisfaction of Miss Cooke. The leaks had widened when J. P. Brennan, a coalition deputy, expressed very frankly his strong disagreement with the way the Government was handling the matter. Then The O'Mahony, a man of great substance throughout the country, an ex-deputy himself of ten years' service, and now high in the inner circles of the Fine Gael organization, wrote a fateful letter to General Mulcahy, leader of that party.

> DEAR GEN. MULCAHY,
>
> Owing to the recent occurrence in Baltinglass regarding the change in the post-office there, I did everything in my power to ensure the fair treatment of the former postmistress, Miss Helen Cooke. You must be aware of the telegram I sent to Mr John Costello.
>
> Taking everything into consideration, I have no other course now but to resign from the Fine Gael organisation. I tried very hard to make justice victorious, but justice has been completely ignored. You personally should know that I could never stand for anything of this kind, and I am more than amazed that full support has not been given by Fine Gael to Miss Cooke.
>
> I deeply regret having to write this letter to you after having worked together in the Dáil for many years.
>
> Yours sincerely,
> O'MAHONY

As if these frontal blows were not crushing enough, five other Government deputies were reported to be considering their resignations. Mr. Costello and his friends began to look round them with haunted eyes. There was confusion in Government ranks, for there seemed a chance that their slender majority in the House might disintegrate like spilled quicksilver.

: 18 :

On the evening of December 21 all the members of the Protest Committee gathered together at Felix O'Neill's to tally the results of the referendum. Long lists of signatures, the names of by far the greater number of voters in the district, were being checked and counterchecked from the sheets of paper attached to a petition, which read:

> We, the registered voters of the postal district of Baltinglass, wish to make it clear that the Minister for Posts and Telegraphs made a misstatement in the Dáil on the night of December 7th and again on December 14th when he said that not the majority of the people of Baltinglass supported Miss Cooke's application for the post of sub-postmistress. We wish to protest against these misstatements and now sign ourselves as firm supporters of Miss Cooke's cause.

Ben Hooper, General Meade Dennis, Luke McDonald, Patrick O'Grady, and Bernie Sheridan were circled purposefully round the O'Neill dining-table while other members of the Protest Committee—indeed, many active workers in the Cooke cause who were not on the Committee—were pouring over the voters' list and checking the collection of signatures against it to make sure there were none in the district who had accidentally been missed. It was a time of great concentration and great gravity, for the supporters of Helen Cooke—even the optimists among them like gentle Ben Hooper and the stubborn warriors like Bernie Sheridan—knew that they were fighting an uphill battle against tremendous odds, even if, in Baltinglass itself, there were nine who backed their little champion for every one who cheered for big Mick Farrell. Not a soul in that room could have anticipated so much of the unexpected as was soon to be theirs, to lift them up from gravity to exultation and from grim concentration to gay forgetfulness.

It was Bernie Sheridan who chanced to look up from his list and saw Felix O'Neill, who had slipped out for a few moments, walk back into the room. Felix walked in quietly, making no fuss, but there was something about the way he carried his padded little figure, a keenness, an awareness, that made Sheridan forget the referendum for a moment and keep his eyes on O'Neill. Later, when he thought about it, Sheridan felt sure that at the time Felix's face was tinted with a telltale flush of excitement and that his brown eyes sparkled and danced; but at the time he only knew that there was something about his friend which fairly called out for attention.

Felix looked round the room, smiling a little to himself as if in anticipation of an effect he was to create. He took a deep breath. Then, in quite a normal tone of voice, he said: "Farrell has resigned."

Sheridan heard him and took it in. Something seemed to catch in his throat. His breathing seemed either to stop or to fade away almost to no breathing at all. Everything was very clear, and he understood perfectly what Felix O'Neill had said, and he saw the General and Ben Hooper and the others going on with their work, but he himself seemed suspended in a moment of space, alone but observant. He saw Ben Hooper, and he heard him, in the very act of reprimanding one of the signature-collectors for not paying attention as his name was being called out.

"Will you pay attention?" Ben was saying, in the same way he might have spoken to one of his boys at the Technical School. "You have missed two people on your list. Why haven't you got their signatures?"

And Felix was still standing there, just inside the door, calm and unflustered, and seeming to look distantly amused.

"Farrell has resigned!" he repeated, a little louder this time, and with a little more stress.

Everybody kept right on with the paper work, refusing to surrender their concentration. Then, suddenly, Ben Hooper looked up, half aware of the significance of Felix's interruption.

"What did you say, Felix?" he asked, still in his headmaster-to-little-boy tone. "There's no time for jokes."

Felix said: "Yes, it's true. Farrell has resigned. It's just been announced on the wireless."

Bernie Sheridan released a great sigh, and he was breathing again. The world rolled on. He began to laugh, very softly, because he couldn't help himself.

And it *was* true. After Felix a steady stream of townsfolk came roaring in, one after the other, neither as calm nor as direct as Felix had been, each thinking himself to be first with the grand news. Ben Hooper and General Dennis rushed off together like eager boys to tell Father Moran and Father Doyle the incredible tidings. People were laughing. Voices rang out, strangely high-pitched and youthful-sounding and excited. None of the Cooke supporters thought to question why Mick Farrell had resigned, for none of them cared. There was much running to and fro, up and down the Main Street, and the frosty winter air echoed with glad, sometimes unintelligible cries. The newspaper reporters, guided by their unerring instinct in such affairs, had deserted their cards and their yarning and their glasses of warm Irish, and had hurried across the street to the centre of the evening's activity. For it was no more than two minutes after Felix O'Neill had broken the news that,

from nowhere it seemed, bottles of whisky were pro-
duced and generously passed round.

"This calls for celebrations," Tom Morrissey
shouted, already a little hoarse. And with that the
meeting was adjourned.

Mrs. Tom Morrissey, a small, pretty woman who
lived near by, knocked at Helen Cooke's door at a
quarter past ten that night. She was still slightly out
of breath when Miss Cooke answered the door.

"Did you hear the news?" Mrs. Morrissey blurted
out excitedly.

"News?" Miss Cooke said. "Would you please
step inside?"

Deputy Patrick Cogan had been a dinner guest of
Helen Cooke and her old Aunt Katie, and now he
was behind his hostess at the door. "Perhaps I had
better leave?" he suggested.

And then Mrs. Morrissey could keep it in no
longer. "Mick Farrell has resigned!" she announced,
all in a rush.

"What's that?" Deputy Cogan said. "Did you—"

"Yes, it's on the wireless," Mrs. Tom Morrissey
said. She was beside herself with excitement and joy.
"He really has resigned."

Helen Cooke said nothing at all. She was stunned.
Her soft cheeks had lost all colour for an instant, and
now it was beginning to flood back.

It was Aunt Katie, that bent and fragile old lady,
who first reacted to the news. "Well, Nellie," she

said, matter-of-factly, "it's about time he gave the job back to you."

Sheridan arrived at Helen Cooke's just as Mrs. Tom Morrissey was leaving, and just as one of the local Gardai came to the door.

"You're wanted on the telephone at the Gardai office, Miss Cooke," the bluecoat said. When the exchange had been moved up the street to Farrell's the Cookes had lost their own telephone; and now Sheridan and Cogan accompanied her to the Gardai office. When she answered her call she found Martin Fallon of the *Irish Press* on the line, speaking from Dublin.

"Will you apply for the job of sub-postmistress now that Farrell has quit?" he asked Miss Cooke.

"I don't know. I'm honestly not sure whether I will or not."

Sheridan, always on guard even when the need for caution seemed to have passed, and not knowing who it was at the other end of the line or what the conversation was about, whispered hoarsely to Miss Cooke. "Don't say too much," he cautioned. "Don't give too much away."

But Miss Cooke hardly heard him. She was already confused at the sudden somersaulting of events. She said good-bye to Martin Fallon, thanking him, and hung up. With Sheridan and Cogan she joined the others who were still tossing the wonderful news back and forth and drinking whisky with it, celebrating the wondrous, unexpected triumph. The rejoicings went on with no interruptions—except for the members of the Protest Committee posing for news photographs with a smiling, white-haired Helen Cooke—until two o'clock in the morning. Perhaps it lasted even later than that, since—as Sheridan frankly admitted later—"I don't remember exactly how it ended, but it was a great victory we were celebrating, and the minor details are best forgotten."

And the minor details *were* forgotten, including one that was hardly merely a detail and far from minor, and what was remembered was the feeling that Aunt Katie, in her innocence, had expressed when she had heard the news: "It's about time he gave the job back to you."

For all the supporters of Miss Cooke, so eager and so glad to see her triumphant, in this joyous hour believed exactly what they wanted to believe, and could not find the catch hidden in the victory.

PART THREE

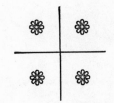

THE

PURSUIT

NEXT MORNING—so terribly bright and cold and clear—brought to the members of the Protest Committee the sickening realization that they had hurried their hopes too quickly along the way. In the papers from Dublin there were letters written by Mick Farrell resigning his post and Jim Everett accepting his resignation.

BALTINGLASS,
Co. WICKLOW
20th Dec., 1950

DEAR MR EVERETT,

I am exceedingly sorry that my appointment as Sub-postmaster of Baltinglass has caused so much controversy and that it has been utilised by your political opponents and certain misguided people to launch an unwarranted attack on you, personally and politically.

My family and I appreciate so much the sterling services which, as a public representative, you have rendered to the nation in general, and to the County Wicklow in particular, that these attacks upon you have caused us much pain and anxiety. I desire to assure you that I would not consciously be the cause of unleashing against you the bitterness and vituperation that has been deliberately directed against you in such unmeasured terms during the past few weeks.

As you know, I was an officer in the L.D.F. during the emergency and am at present an officer of the F.C.A. I hold testimonials from my superior officers (who, incidentally, recommended me for the Baltinglass post) which express in high terms their regard for my service and efficiency. It is an honour to me to wear an Irish officer's uniform and to be privileged to serve my country in any danger that may arise. Holding these views, therefore, I am particularly anxious that the uniform which I proudly wear should not become associated with, or be in any way besmirched by, the violent abuse and illegal acts for which your political opponents have been responsible following my appointment.

Having reviewed the whole position I have now come to the conclusion that I should resign my position as Sub-Postmaster of Baltinglass in order that my name and my family's will not be further used as a cover from which to launch base and undeserved attacks upon you and so that, as an officer in the nation's Defence Forces, I may not even remotely appear to associate my status with the brawling atmosphere in which certain persons delight.

I hope you will forgive me for taking this decision, but, believe me, I have been actuated solely by my high regard for you, my appreciation of your unstinted service to the people of the County Wicklow and for the honour of my uniform. I know it looks odd that I am eligible to wear the uniform of the Defence Forces of my own country, and am free to die in its service, but am denied an appointment to a small position in a country sub-post-office. However, one must not expect logic when abuse and vilification have taken control of the situation.

I thank you for your confidence in me and I close by again tendering my deep regret that you should be occasioned such worry and annoyance.

Yours sincerely,
MICHAEL FARRELL

DUBLIN
21st December, 1950

DEAR MR FARRELL,

I have received your letter of the 20th instant tendering your resignation from the position of Sub-Postmaster of Baltinglass. I regret that you have taken this decision, but I appreciate your sentiments and the manly spirit which actuated you. I should like you to understand clearly that from the standpoint of qualifications, you were eminently fitted for the post, and that your decision to resign is in no way related to your ability and general suitability for the position. As your decision is your own free choice, I must accept it as such.

I should, perhaps, add that your appointment has thrown into bold relief the long-established practice of making appointments to these posts. For some time past I have been considering, with my Department, the adoption of a new method of selecting candidates for such appointments. The present method, which we inherited from our predecessors, is open to many objections, inasmuch as it provides opportunities for candidates to seek political influence in respect of such appointments, as is evidenced by the fact that even in your own case members of parties supporting the Government, and four members of the Fianna Fáil Party, felt impelled to make representations to me on your behalf. Ironically enough, the Deputies of the Fianna Fáil Party complained when the candidate whom they recommended was appointed.

I dislike intensely a system of appointment where political influence can be used in the filling of such positions and I intend at the earliest opportunity to introduce arrangements whereby appointments to sub-post-offices will be made by an official interview board which will be instructed to disqualify at once any candidate who attempts to

use political influence in the furtherance of his or
her candidature.

Yours sincerely,

JAMES EVERETT

There then, for all to judge, were the viewpoints
of both Mick Farrell, past sub-postmaster of Baltinglass, and Jim Everett, Minister for Posts and Telegraphs; for not only did they write the letters—so
complete, so reasonable, and so modest—to one another, not only did they send copies to the Dublin
daily papers, but the Minister also made them available to Radio Éireann. Perhaps, in forwarding the
copies of these letters to the press, the two widely
separated colleagues had taken their cue from the
Protest Committee itself, but the radio idea was original and previously untried in the Baltinglass battle.

In the reading of these letters the Protest Committee saw at once that the important thing about the one
from Mr. Everett was not so much what he said as
what he did not say. He had made no mention in it
about handing the newly vacant position over to the
remaining claimant for it.

Mick Farrell, it was true, no longer was an obstacle
in Helen Cooke's way; but that good lady was still
without her job.

: 2 :

IT was clear—too clear—that the battle on Helen Cooke's behalf was not over. The unrestrained joy of her supporters which had held sway the night before dissipated into doubt, and from doubt into grave meditation. The faces of the members of the Protest Committee grew long and thoughtful as—after word-by-word study of the Minister's letter—they word by word lost hope. On Friday, the day after the premature celebration, an emergency meeting was called to discuss events as they now presented themselves. The meeting started early and lasted until late. And it was Ben Hooper who summarized the situation.

"Our agitation for Miss Cooke," he said, his soft leprechaun's eyes serious and sad, "will still have to go on. All we have ever had to fight with at any time was the publicity—keeping the thing before the eyes of the public. And, indeed, that's all we have now. We have nothing against Farrell—sure, and he's out of the picture at any rate. We are now fighting against the Government pure and simple."

There was a grim, grunted chorus of approval.

"It's the people versus the Government," Ben Hooper continued, warming to his theme. "So now we have to bring our case *to* the people of Eire. The question is: how are we going to do it?"

Jim McCann rose awkwardly to his feet, as if he were not entirely sure of himself. "Why not hire out other public-address systems like what we done before?" He looked round at his colleagues for approval, but they looked back at him with polite blankness, as if they were not expecting anything very practical or very dramatic. "Why not put the p-a systems on cars," Jim McCann said, elaborating his idea, "and do a tour of the country? We could tell the people that way, I do believe."

"Well!" said General Dennis, breathing out suddenly. "Well!"

And Sheridan nodded his head slowly, slowly, sucking in his underlip the while. And Ben Hooper's soft eyes shone brightly. And John A. Doyle whistled a tuneless little note and said: "Now *that's* an idea! And we can collect signatures as we go."

: 3 :

OF course, there were other viewpoints, in addition to those of Mick Farrell, the ex-sub-postmaster, and of Jim Everett, the Minister for Posts and Telegraphs, and they did not long remain concealed. There was, by way of example, the viewpoint of Miss Trasa MacGeehan in Dublin, and an interesting one it was.

"The Committee of the Dublin Section of the

Baltinglass Protest Committee," she announced, "have to date received mail from every single county in Ireland. No one can claim now that this protest is not nationwide, nor can it be claimed that our work on Helen Cooke's behalf has a political slant, for no member of the committee has any affiliations whatever with political parties. We undertook this work purely in the interest of Christian charity and patriotism."

When pressed—although not *hard* pressed—by reporters on the Friday after Mick Farrell resigned, General Meade Dennis said what he thought about the affair as well.

"The committee," he declared with grave emphasis, "has fought the fight with clean hands. Our fight was against an action which strikes at the very root of democratic government." Then, to indicate that the battle was not yet over, he added: "It was said to me the other day by a man of very great personality * that 'anybody can raise a mob to break windows, but it takes great men to raise a mob to mend them.' Baltinglass intends to mend them."

* There were some who suspected, but none who were sure, that the General's reference was to none other than Eamon de Valera.

:4:

ITEM from the *Irish Times*, Saturday, December 23:

The reaction in Baltinglass yesterday to the announcement that Mr Michael Farrell, postmaster
of eleven days, has resigned the post was one of
surprise, writes an *Irish Times* reporter who spent
the day there. There were no celebrations. Indeed,
the one impression was one of unusual quiet of an
Irish township on the eve of Christmas.

The dispute over the Baltinglass Post Office appointment will leave its mark on the hitherto ami-
cable relations of the eight hundred inhabitants of
the district. Although it is stressed continually by
the supporters of Miss Helen Cooke that there is
no personal animosity against the family of Michael Farrell, the events of the past few weeks undoubtedly have created a bitterness that will be
hard to eradicate.

While it would appear that the resignation of
the new postmaster caught the Protest Committee
off-balance from yesterday's happening, it will not
make any difference to the plan of campaign which
had already been drawn up. The attitude of the
Committee, summed up in a supplied statement
after its meeting yesterday, was that the resigna-

tion was not the achievement for which the campaign had begun.

The Committee, individually and collectively,
states that until Miss Cooke is installed as postmistress they will carry the campaign into the Dáil,
into the houses of the people of the country, and
anywhere they think they can further the cause for
which they are fighting.

Their attitude is that Miss Cooke should automatically be appointed postmistress with the resignation of the only person who applied with her for
the position last April. Miss Cooke, when asked if
she would apply for the position again, following
the announcement that the post was vacant, said
that she would not make any comment.

If, as would seem the normal procedure, a notice
is placed in the window of Mr Farrell's premises
inviting applicants for the position, it is considered
highly unlikely that anybody else in Baltinglass
would seek the post. In the unlikely eventuality of
the Minister appointing anyone else, the campaign
would be pursued just as strenuously a spokesman
said yesterday.

The "Protest Committee"—as it has come to be
known—when the news of the resignation was con-
firmed, held an emergency meeting which lasted
the afternoon.

At the office of Mr Michael Farrell, where two
officials of the Department from Dublin have been

instructing him in the duties of postmaster since his appointment, business continued as usual. Last night, the officials, who had been instructed to carry on until they received further orders, received word that they were to remain on. Mr Farrell, although he has resigned, may continue to receive the benefit of their experience.

During the afternoon a considerable amount of postal business was transacted. The letterbox at the side of the shop was emptied while an *Irish Times* reporter was present, and contained a number of letters.

Michael Farrell refused to comment on his future plans, nor would he say anything about his resignation. His attitude was that when he thought the time opportune he would have plenty to say. He described as "lies" that the working of the post-office had been brought to a standstill through the non-usage by the followers of Miss Cooke.

He would not, he said, accept any alternative position, "even if I am offered £1000 a year." His decision to resign, he stated, was taken against the wishes of his supporters, who expressed their faith in him and pressed him to change his mind.

Commenting on the claims made by Miss Cooke's followers that the referendum of the people in the postal area had shown an overwhelming majority in their favour, he said that it was not a true indication of the people's wishes as it was not actually a census of the people who received post, but of anybody who happened to be home at the time.

The meeting of the "Protest Committee" was attended by Mr P. Cogan, T.D., who stated that he would press in the Dáil for private time to discuss the motion tabled jointly by himself and Mr T. Brennan, F.F., that a select committee of the House be set up to inquire into the whole circumstances of the appointment.

The following statement was made at the end of the meeting:

> This committee was formed to voice the protest of the people of Baltinglass at the grave injustice done to Miss Cooke by the Minister for Posts and Telegraphs in not appointing her to the vacancy arising in the post-office on the resignation of Miss Katie Cooke. It will be dissolved when that injustice has been rectified.
>
> This Committee once again wishes to stress that at no time has any question of party politics influenced them in their actions, and deplores the harm that may have resulted to Michael Farrell and his family through the Minister's action.

The sentiments expressed in the statement were reiterated by Major-Gen. M. E. Dennis—"There is no question of Michael Farrell or his family being victimized," he said. "I personally will not stand out against Farrell. They have always been good tenants of mine."

Mr B. Sheridan, a member of the committee, criticized the action of Mr Everett, as Minister responsible for wireless broadcasting, in giving the full texts of the letters on Mr Farrell's resignation in the 10 o'clock news on Thursday night in full, and before they had been released to the Press, when, previously, Radio Éireann had ignored the developments at Baltinglass. "He was only justifying himself," he said.

The O'Mahony, former Fine Gael T.D. for Wicklow, and a member of the West Wicklow Executive of the Party, has received no acknowledgement yet to his letter of resignation as a protest against the appointment. Mr Felix O'Neill has also resigned, but did not send any letter.

The Committee is awaiting the next move from the Minister. According to Rule 28 of the regulations governing sub-postmasters and postmistresses,

A sub-postmaster who wishes to resign his appointment must give three months' notice of his intention to do so, otherwise he may be called upon to pay any expenses which may be involved in providing for his duties. He is required to sign an undertaking to this effect when taking up his duties.

Mr Michael Farrell, so far as can be ascertained, was not required to give the stipulated notice. Compensation for the money he has expended on constructing the post-office at the back of his father's drapery shop may be paid by the Ministry.

Until the whole position is clarified by the Minister, the committee will go ahead with their formulated plans. A meeting will be held in the Mansion House, Dublin, on January 5th, at which Miss Cooke, Mr Cogan and others will speak. The petition for signatures in Dublin and other parts of the country is still being pushed forward.

When the news of Michael Farrell's resignation was announced, Miss Cooke early yesterday said: "We could never have pulled through without the help of the townspeople, who, from the very beginning, have realized the very grave issues at stake, and were determined to stand by until they have seen this injustice exposed throughout the country."

She praised the work of the Protest Committee and said that it was done at serious inconvenience to themselves. She hoped that the knowledge gained in their fight against injustice would recompense them somewhat for their endeavours.

: 5 :

By now people all over Eire had lined up on one side or the other of the battle, and "letters to the editor" columns of the daily newspapers were crammed with the subject and little else. Opinions were very freely expressed for all to see, although now and again from behind the protective anonymity of a set of initials or a nom de plume. One such appeared in the *Irish Times* on December 20.

Sir,

Now the tumult and shouting about l'Affaire Baltinglass has somewhat subsided, I trust a few words from a disinterested spectator may not come amiss.

I am free from any political bias in this connection, but I do think that the people of Baltinglass must be envied at this particular moment, when the whole world is in such a chaotic state. They must surely live in Utopia. There are obviously no other problems upsetting their equilibrium except the appointment of a postmaster. There are no housing problems, no hungry children, no sick and hungry people in need of attention in this community. Obviously none of these things appear to have existed in Baltinglass for some considerable time. Otherwise, the worthy townsfolk, of all shades of political opinion and social status, would have done something concrete about it.

Suppose that Baltinglass has other problems, such as I have mentioned above, would not the people who have spent their time sitting on manholes and knocking down telegraph poles be much better employed in using their energies for the benefit of those unfortunate people of their town who need a better way of life, than in making a public exhibition of themselves in a misguided effort to focus the light of publicity on just one injustice? Are there not many more extant, in Baltinglass—and all over the world—more worthy of such stupendous effort?

Yours, etc.,
"La Petite Chose"

Dublin
December 17*th*, 1950

In the same issue of the same paper another letter was published.

Sir,

I would be very grateful if you would clear up one matter, once and for all, connected with the post-office dispute at Baltinglass, which has got wide publicity and has led to much confusion—*viz.*, Miss Helen Cooke, the ex-postmistress is a Roman Catholic, belonging to an old and respected family in my parish. At the same time, I would like you to make known that Mr Desmond James Cullen (chemist) is also a Roman Catholic, living in my parish, and belongs to a highly respected Tipperary family.

Both families have members in the religious life.

Yours, etc.,

REV. PATRICK DOYLE, P.P., V.F.

PAROCHIAL HOUSE, BALTINGLASS, CO. WICKLOW

December 19th, 1950

And then, the very next day, in the same column:

SIR,

Your correspondent, *La Petite Chose*, after careful meditation, has come to the conclusion that the only effective way to defeat the Baltinglass people's fight for justice is to belittle the whole affair. He asks if they have no other worries such as bad housing, sickness, hunger, etc. The answer is that, in common with other towns and villages, they have all those problems, but that did not prevent them from turning aside to go to the rescue of two small women who had lived quietly in their midst for many years, and who, in the opinion of the people, had been gravely wronged. The men who rushed to the aid of the Cooke family were plain citizens of this State. Some were engaged in business, some were farmers, and many were just ordinary workers depending on their weekly wages. But they all united together in defence of the rights of a fellow citizen.

The position in question may be only a minor one in the State, but to the Cooke family it was their means of livelihood. Not one sound argument was advanced for the transfer of the post office, and I am satisfied that the whole nation stands behind the people of Baltinglass in their fight for justice.

The whole incident proves, if proof were needed, that the instincts of our people are fundamentally sound and decent, and that the ideals of justice and fair play are still warmly cherished in the Irish heart. The petition of protest sponsored by the Dublin section of the Baltinglass Protest Committee is being enthusiastically supported, and signatures are pouring in from all parts of the country to Miss MacGeehan's office at 7 Harcourt Terrace, Dublin. The fight will continue until justice is done, and out of the struggle there will emerge a cleaner and better political and administrative system for the whole nation.

Yours, etc.,

PATRICK COGAN, T.D.

DÁIL ÉIREANN, LEINSTER HOUSE, DUBLIN
December 20th, 1950

On December 23 the following:

SIR,

Having read in your issue of December 22nd
that the recently appointed sub-postmaster to Baltinglass Post Office has resigned, I feel that, had
he done so in the start, I would have been very
glad to congratulate him. But, having read his
letter of resignation to the Minister for Posts and
Telegraphs, I am disgusted at all the insinuations
which it contains. Any worry or annoyance which,
it states, the Minister has suffered, has only been
caused by the Minister himself. A great injustice
has been done, and that injustice stands until recti-
fied.

Yours, etc.,
THE O'MAHONY

GRANGECON, CO. WICKLOW

And again:

SIR,

The implication expressed in *La Petite Chose's*
letter seems to me to have a striking resemblance
to the exception taken to Mary Magdalene's waste
of valuable ointment on Our Lord's feet, and his
answer is equally applicable in this case, "The poor
always ye have with you." But the opportunity of
effective action in suppressing an act of gross injustice must be acted on promptly and not let go

by default. Otherwise, once a Government gets into power, by making specious promises it has no intention of implementing, it will be able to ride roughshod over all the people's rights to liberty, fair play and justice.

Yours, etc.,

R. F. HEWSON

GARDEN COTTAGE, ADARE
December 22nd, 1950

And nothing could be clearer from the letters, from the talk in the public houses, from the continued interest of editors—in Eire and abroad—that indeed the men in high places who had sent the Gardai down to Baltinglass in force to wipe out the controversy had failed totally to do so; and the resignation—for whatever reason he may have had—of Michael Farrell had, instead of ending the battle, spread the flame and heaped new fuel upon it.

:6:

WHO would have thought that four small cars, with a mere sixteen people in them, could have caused the conquest of a nation? Who would have thought that Jim McCann's hesitant suggestion about attaching the public-address equipment to cars and sending them over all of Eire to spread the Baltinglass message could have the results it had? Yet, from the first, the idea was received by the Committee and Miss Cooke's rank-and-file supporters with gusto and glee. Soup Doyle *insisted* that the Committee accept the use of his Vauxhall for the purpose; and Luke McDonald with his Ford Anglia, Ben Hooper with his Ford Prefect, and Cecil Gale with his Morris were just as anxious to donate the wear and tear of their vehicles to the cause. When the public-address equipment was hired—from a sympathizer at half the usual rate of rental—and mounted on the cars all was ready for the grand tour of enlightenment and propaganda.

And then, with the cheers and blessings of their fellow townsmen ringing pleasantly in their ears, they set out along the icy roads, shooting off in four directions at once—to the distant west, the far south, the neighbouring east, and the deep north—like the lopsided spokes in a lopsided wheel. And soon the reports were coming back to Baltinglass of their progress, of Bernie Sheridan and his team, for example, setting up branch protest-committees in Drumlish; in Kiltimagh; in Roscommon and Castlereagh; in Ballinasloe, Claremorris, and Loughrea. Or of Ben Hooper and his helpers being received in state and with enthusiastic promises of aid by the Mayor of Cork, by the Mayor of Waterford, and by the Mayor of Limerick; and of setting up protest committees in Kilkenny, Killarney, Tralee, Tarbert, Limerick, and Dungarvan. Or of Des Cullen, in the south, speaking

over his p-a system as follows: "People of Wexford
—this is Baltinglass calling. We ask for your assistance in our fight for justice. January 1st is signature
day. Send your signature to Miss T. MacGeehan,
7 Harcourt Terrace, Dublin. *You* may be thrown out
of your job next. Our fight is your fight. Form a committee in your town and help fight for fair play. We
request you to assist us in having Miss Cooke reinstated in the post-office by signing the petition when
supporters approach you. This fight is not political."
Or of printed handbills being given out that read, under the heading: BALTINGLASS DEMANDS CLEAN AD-
MINISTRATION:

> Baltinglass Post Office has become a National af-
> fair.
>
> Are you on the side of justice and honest ad-
> ministration or will you support dishonest totali-
> tarian methods? What happened to Miss Cooke in
> Baltinglass may happen to any servant of the state
> in any town in Ireland to-morrow.
>
> YOU can put matters right and make it clear
> once and for all that the PEOPLE OF IRELAND stand
> united against dishonest administration and politi-
> cal graft.

The signatures came by the thousand; and new
protest-committees took root in Collooney, Portlaoise,
and Killorglin; and the word spread and everywhere
Irishmen flocked to the Cooke banner. The fact is

that of all the teams only Bernie Sheridan's ran into a single hostile reception, and that was by a man on the highway between Westport and Galway, on the west coast, who honked the horn of his car and shouted after them hoarsely: "Up Everett! Up Everett!" Meanwhile, at a meeting of the County Kildare Association of I.R.A. representatives of Counties Kildare, Laois, Offaly, Wicklow, and Meath, held at Droichead Nua, the following resolution was unanimously passed:

That we, the County Kildare Brigade Old I.R.A. protest in the strongest possible terms at the flagrant injustice of the methods of the Minister for Posts and Telegraphs in the matter of the appointment of the Postmaster of Baltinglass. This Association represents the men who fought for equal rights and justice for all the people of the thirty-two County Republic.

Editorials in favour of Miss Cooke blossomed in the pages of the papers in the wake of the Baltinglass visitors. For example, the *Longford Leader* said:

The Minister obviously walked into a nest of trouble and no amount of diplomacy will recover the position. Maybe it was good that it happened. Public appointments should be subject to public scrutiny and public protest where necessary. That's democracy at work.

Indeed, and in every way the two-thousand-mile tour became an electric charge through the country. In Dublin high Government officials read reports of the four-pronged campaign with growing uneasiness and embarrassment as the truth came home to even them—that Mick Farrell's resignation had come too late, and was not enough in itself to appease the people of Eire. And when Mr. Everett, the Minister for Posts and Telegraphs, chose this moment to go to the hospital for a stomach operation there was little doubt that many of his colleagues would have liked to have gone with him.

: 7 :

BEFORE Mr. Everett took himself off to his hospital retreat he made it abundantly clear that the post-office of Baltinglass, vacant for the second time in a fortnight, would be filled in a way to bar criticism. First, the position would be advertised—in Michael Farrell's window—and then, from the new candidates, the appointment would be made by an official interview-board especially set up for the purpose. "And," added the Minister, "the interview board will be instructed to disqualify at once any candidate who attempts to use political influence in the furtherance of his or her candidature." Finally it was announced by the Minister's Department that the closing date for applications was January the 6th.

Helen Cooke, at this point, found herself in an embarrassing position. Even though Mick Farrell's resignation had been accepted, her former rival still operated the official village post-office until his successor could be selected. Inevitably, and under the warlike circumstances, the rift between the two feuding families had become total. She could not bring herself to walk into the Farrell establishment and ask the young man for an application form. "Indeed, and I couldn't give him the satisfaction," she said stubbornly.

Thus it was that, just after the New Year, she and two of her friends from Baltinglass, Lily Kehoe and Mary Whelan, visited Dublin together. They walked past one of the city post-offices, and Miss Cooke nudged Miss Kehoe.

"Lily," she said, and paused.

"Yes?"

"Lily, would you ever mind going into the post-office for me and doing the asking?"

"Sure, I'd be glad," said Miss Kehoe promptly.

The three women pushed through the post-office door and looked round. When she saw that the place was empty of customers Miss Cooke sighed softly. She stood aside with Miss Whelan while Miss Kehoe stepped up to the counter.

"Please, could I have a form applying for a sub-post-office?" she asked the man behind the wire.

He peered out at her. "And what would the post-office be?" he asked, with purely technical interest.

"In the country," Miss Kehoe said, purposely vague.

"Yes, but what town?"

Miss Kehoe shot a quick, nervous glance over her shoulder at Helen Cooke.

"Baltinglass," she said, her voice dropping to a whisper.

The post-office man was visibly jolted out of his indifference. Indeed, he could hardly have reacted more violently if Miss Kehoe had pointed a gun at him. He stared at her, not wanting to believe what he had heard. Then the corners of his mouth crept almost imperceptibly downward. He shook his head reprovingly. "Well," he said, "if I were you I wouldn't stoop so low as to apply for that. And even if you did get the post it won't do you any good or stay with you for long."

Miss Kehoe stared back at him for a moment in surprise. Then she threw her head back, and her laughter filled the room. The post-office man was obviously an ally! He continued to eye her distastefully. Presently, when her laughter faded, she leaned towards him confidentially. "It's all right," she said. "Indeed, and the form is for Miss Cooke herself."

:8:

ITEM from the *Irish Press*, January 8:

MR FARRELL MAY STAND FOR DÁIL

Many T.D.'s, including Mr P. Cogan (Ind.), have received copies of a statement issued on the advice of a committee of his supporters by Mr Michael Farrell, who was appointed sub-postmaster at Baltinglass by Mr Everett, Minister for Posts and Telegraphs, and who later resigned.

Mr Farrell in the statement thanks all the people from different parts of Ireland who had offered him support in his fight against a "political combination of English ranchers and Fianna Fáil supporters who have used this case as a cloak for their own political interests and objected to his appointment which was awarded on merit in the town where he was born and reared."

One could appreciate, it continued, sympathy from generous, kindly Irish people, particularly those who did not realize what some political parties would do to further their own interests and attack a political opponent.

He said that his father was not a wealthy man but had only the sort of business which "one would expect in any country town—a mixed business in a small way." His "large farm consists of 18 acres, seven of which are bog land."

Miss Cooke, in fact, owned freehold property in Baltinglass which was more valuable than his father's property which carried a very heavy ground rent.

"Would it not be more in keeping with Christian principles to appoint a young man on whose shoulders the responsibility of a family may one day rest?" the statement continues.

"Many prominent people have appealed to me to contest the next Parliamentary elections in my own constituency—not in Cork, as suggested to Miss Cooke—and even though I have not up to the present identified myself with any political party, I am carefully considering the matter."

Concluding, Mr Farrell said that Miss Cooke had the support of "the Cromwellians and a few of the wealthy shopkeepers, but 60 per cent. of the plain Irish people of Baltinglass are opposed to Miss Cooke holding the position."

Mr B. Sheridan, a member of the Baltinglass Protest Committee, told an *Irish Press* reporter on Saturday that allegations that there was political influence behind the protest were utterly ridiculous.

The people, said Mr Sheridan, were far too familiar with the facts of the case to accept such a statement.

Any money used for the campaign in support of Miss Cooke was subscribed by the townspeople of Baltinglass, he said. Those who gave money in-

cluded Labour Party * supporters and followers of
the Fine Gael Party. Many other offers of money
were turned down by the committee. Names and
addresses of subscribers were available for scrutiny
and the Labour Party would, perhaps, be shocked
to learn some of them.

Six hundred signatures claimed by Mr Farrell
to have been collected in his favour could not have
come from the Baltinglass area, Mr Sheridan al-
leged, and it was common knowledge in the town
that on Wednesday last a car visited Stratford,
which is not in the Baltinglass postal district, collecting signatures for Mr Farrell. Stratford,
though in Baltinglass parish, has its own post-
office.

The referendum carried out after Christmas by
Miss Cooke's supporters in the postal district of
Baltinglass was available and could be seen by anyone who doubted that 87 per cent. of the townspeople were not in favour of the former sub-postmistress.

Up to yesterday 13,000 signatories were received for the protest circulated in regard to the
non-appointment of Miss Cooke.

The committee is prepared to submit the names
of the signatories for public examination; also
those received in the referendum which was con-
fined to Baltinglass postal area.

* Mr. Everett's party.

In regard to Mr Farrell's claim that he had obtained 700 signatures to his memorial, the committee challenged him to take the same steps for its examination by the public.

: 9 :

THE days passed (Sheridan said) and the weeks passed and the battle itself seemed to be settling down to a period of strange suspended animation, with neither side putting up an attack. It was as if both sides wanted peace, but were too proud to make the first move. The month of January was almost over— it was Friday, the 26th—when Joe Doyle came running across the Main Street, risking a bad fall on the ice, and into my public house.

"Con Dempsey, the postmaster from Naas," he says, "has gone into Miss Cooke's with Noel Slattery." Joe was out of breath from his running, and his colour was high.

"Well!" I say. And I ran out into the street without stopping for my coat, and heard Maureen calling to me about it, but I didn't turn back. Not then! Miss Cooke had been advised by the Protest Committee that if anyone came from the other side, or from the Post Office, she should not see him or talk to him until such time as someone from the Committee had investigated and approved of whoever it was. I had to

get down there and act for the Committee as a scruti-
neer. I ran all the way down the Main Street and
along the Mill Street, and when I got to Miss Cooke's
I stopped for a moment outside the door and caught
my breath. Then I knocked at the door, and Miss
Katie Cooke answered it.

"Nellie has gone upstairs, Mr. Sheridan," she says
to me, whispering it soft and low. I nodded to her to
show I had heard.

Then I said hello to the two men from the post-
office in Naas, whom I did not know in person, although they were well known to me by reputation. I
was aware that they were all right. "What is it you've
come for?" I say. "Is there any way I can help?"

"We've come to see Miss Cooke," Con Dempsey
says. He looked at me and I looked at him, and I
think the two of us both liked what we saw.

"All right," I say, and I went up and told Miss
Cooke it was time to come down.

Con Dempsey smiled at her, and he says: "Con-
gratulations, Miss Cooke. You are the new postmistress!"

"Indeed!" Miss Cooke says, her face pink and
pleased. "Indeed!" she says again. Then, aware that
we had never officially met, Miss Cooke introduced
me to Con Dempsey, and we shook hands. Even in
my excitement at this great victory I was wondering
what had happened to the interview board Mr. Everett had promised, since Miss Cooke had certainly

not been called before it—and here she was, sub-post-mistress of Baltinglass!

"I'm going to inform the Protest Committee," I say to Con Dempsey. "Now," I say. It was wonderful news, marvellous news, and I felt I could keep it to myself no longer.

Con Dempsey lost his smile in a hurry. "No!" he says. "You're not! Not until I inform Mr. Farrell. Give me ten minutes," he says. "Play it fair."

"All right," I say, reluctant.

Con Dempsey stepped towards the door, and then, as though he was remembering something important, he turned back again to Helen Cooke. There was a peculiar, embarrassed look on his face. "That stamp," he says to Miss Cooke, "BALTINGLASS DEMANDS CLEAN ADMINISTRATION—the one that has been stamped on all the letters in red ink," he says. "The use of it will have to cease."

Miss Cooke looked at him with a smile on her lips so small you could hardly see it. Very innocently she says: "And why will it, Mr. Dempsey? Surely our Government could not feel that there was any reference to them in what the stamp says? Surely they could not feel that they had not acted correctly?"

Con Dempsey coughed. He turned on a little colour, and, saying no more, went up the Mill Street to tell Mick Farrell that a new appointee was to take his place.

Ten minutes later I ran back up the way I had

come. I ran up and told Ben Hooper the wonderful news, and the two of us telephoned General Dennis and arranged a celebration for that night. Then I went home and told Maureen.

"It isn't true, Bernie!" Maureen says to me. "Not after all this time!"

It hardly seemed possible, but we had finally won the battle. We had got justice at last for Nellie Cooke.

: 10 :

AFTER that—with Miss Cooke and the Protest Committee happy and victorious—Mr. Costello and Mr. Everett and the important men in the Government clearly yearned to forget the Battle of Baltinglass. One indication of their eagerness to bury the affair in oblivion was the reply given to an inquisitive press, which wanted further details of Miss Cooke's appointment, by an official of the Government Information Bureau.

"This is just another post-office appointment," he said, as blandly as only a civil servant can, "and it is not customary to make any statement or to disclose how many applications were received." When questioned about Mr. Everett's promise of a few weeks before to the effect that in future *all* post-office appointments would be made by an official interview-board (and when it was pointed out to him that Miss Cooke had not been called before such a board) he simply shrugged and let silence speak for him. Yes, undoubtedly the outcome of the battle had been a very great embarrassment to the losing side, and they would have welcomed the chance to turn permanently to other matters. For a very short time, indeed, they were happily lulled into Lethe, but this happiness was rudely disturbed in the Dáil itself—and, ironically, on that most romantic of days, which custom has dedicated to lovers and St. Valentine—when Mr. Cogan asked a question.

Extract from the Official Report, *Parliamentary Debates, Dáil Éireann*, February 14:

TRANSFER OF SUB-POST-OFFICE

Mr Cogan asked the Minister for Posts and Telegraphs if he will state the total cost of transferring the sub-post-office at Baltinglass from Miss Cooke's premises to those of Mr Farrell and of re-transferring it back again.

MINISTER FOR SOCIAL WELFARE (Mr Norton) (for the Minister of Posts and Telegraphs): The total cost of transferring the sub-post-office at Baltinglass from Miss Cooke's premises to those of Mr Farrell and of re-transferring it was £213.

MR MACENTEE: Oh!

Mʀ Sᴍɪᴛʜ: Up the Republic!

Mʀ MᴀᴄEɴᴛᴇᴇ: That, surely, is an understatement.

Mʀ Cᴏɢᴀɴ: Can the Minister state if this sum which he has mentioned includes the cost of bringing fifty Guards down to Baltinglass for the transfer, and of maintaining an extra force there? Does it include also the cost of compensation for the Farrell family?

Mʀ Nᴏʀᴛᴏɴ: The sum which I have mentioned is the total cost of transferring the sub-post-office at Baltinglass from Miss Cooke's premises to those of Mr Farrell, and of re-transferring the post-office again. That is the information which the Deputy asked for, and that is the information which he has got.

Mʀ Cᴏɢᴀɴ: Does that include the compensation for the Farrell family?

Aɴ Cᴇᴀɴɴ Cᴏᴍʜᴀɪʀʟᴇ: The Deputy did not ask that.

Mʀ Nᴏʀᴛᴏɴ: The Deputy did not ask that question and compensation is no element in the answer.

Mʀ MᴀᴄEɴᴛᴇᴇ: Everybody, with any knowledge of this case, knows that that is a gross understatement.

Aɴ Cᴇᴀɴɴ Cᴏᴍʜᴀɪʀʟᴇ: That, surely, is not a supplementary.

Mʀ MᴀᴄEɴᴛᴇᴇ: It is a corrective.

DR O'HIGGINS: A fallacious one.

MR MACENTEE: Not any more than the Minister's.

Mr Cogan asked the Minister for Posts and Telegraphs if Mr Michael Farrell, before being appointed sub-postmaster for Baltinglass, had satisfied him that the premises which he proposed to use as post-office were not part of premises licensed under the Intoxicating Liquor Acts.

MR NORTON: I would refer the Deputy to the answer to the question on the same subject given to him on 14th December last.

MR COGAN: Is the Minister aware that it has since been proved beyond question that the premises which were opened as a sub-post-office were part of licensed premises and are still licensed?

MR DILLON: Surely, the galloper should finish galloping.

MR NORTON: Whatever the legal position may be I cannot determine that. It can only be determined by the courts. The factual position is that the part of the premises used as a post-office was segregated to the satisfaction of the Post-Office Department in the grocery portion of the premises. The courts can decide the other matter. I do not propose to pass any judgment upon it.

And, alas! in early March one who had been a stalwart figure in the fighting of the battle died, in the person of Father Doyle, the parish priest, and the town of Baltinglass stood still, deep in mourning and in sorrow. The day of the funeral, mindful of the day the Gardai swept the stone slab clear, was cold, and the sleet bit into the faces of the villagers who climbed up Baltinglass Hill to see their old, loved friend laid to his last rest. And later they trudged down the steep hillside, some of them letting tears mingle with the melting sleet, and walked past the drawn blinds of the shops and into their homes, rinsed for the day of worldly thoughts and worldly deeds.

Yet even then there was no end to the affair that, at first, Mr. Costello had thought a trifle. For the turmoil and the strife that had been aroused over a minor Government post in the tiny town of Baltinglass, and in the defence of two women—one old and ailing, the other tiny, white-haired, and faithful—and that had grown and grown and grown until the entire country had taken sides, was to end in a way that nobody, and certainly not Mr. Costello, could possibly have foreseen. Perhaps never before had such a seeming triviality inspired so democratic an adventure. Perhaps never again would the people of an entire nation join together fiercely to right so small a wrong, and in the doing of it move the nation itself.

For, in the end, the Battle of Baltinglass did, in a way, move the Republic of Eire.

Item from the London *Daily Express*, a morning newspaper, of May 5, 1951:

The political storm that began with the appointment of a postmaster in the little Co. Wicklow village of Baltinglass ended last night with the resignation of the Eire Government.

A General Election is to be held on May 30.

The row started when a man was appointed to the job that Miss Helen Cooke had done for fourteen years. It spread to the Dáil—Eire's Parliament—and an ex-Minister was suspended during a rowdy debate.

In the end, forty-six-year-old Miss Cooke got her job back; but more cracks appeared in the Government—over the planned health service. The Government quarrelled with the Independents, whose votes helped to keep it in power.

And last night Premier John Costello gave up the struggle.

Indeed, and that is how the affair came to a timely end—for all, that is, except Mr. Gaffney, the ballader, who let his brain run riot and his pen grow hot.

The job of sub-postmaster or mistress, as might be,
Is not exactly one that leads to wealth and luxury;
But Korea was a picnic and Tobruk was just a pup
To the row the day the linesmen came to take the cable up.

Now the case has gone to U.N.O., and we're waiting for the day

When Truman, Attlee, and McBride will come
   along and say,
"Get back behind your parallel, drop atom bombs
   and gas,
And respect the bound'ries and the laws of
   Sov'reign Baltinglass."

But there was none in Eire, by then, not fully conversant with the facts of the case; and the facts were
incredible enough without quarrelling with Mr. Gaffney's fancy.

A NOTE ON THE TYPE
IN WHICH THIS BOOK IS SET

This book is set in Linotype CASLON, a modern
adaptation of a type designed by the first William
Caslon (1692–1766). The Caslon face has had
two centuries of ever-increasing popularity in the
United States—it is of interest to note that the
first copies of the Declaration of Independence
and the first paper currency distributed to the
citizens of the new-born nation were printed in
this type face.

COMPOSED, PRINTED, AND BOUND
BY KINGSPORT PRESS, INC.,
KINGSPORT, TENNESSEE